BORN OF STRUGGLE, LIVING IN HOPE

The Anarcho-Punk Lives of the Centro Iberico, 1971–1983

Nick Soulsby

PM

Born of Struggle, Living in Hope: The Anarcho-Punk Lives of the Centro Iberico, 1971–1983
© 2026 Nick Soulsby
This edition © 2026 PM Press

ISBN: 979-8-88744-122-1 (paperback)
ISBN: 979-8-88744-123-8 (ebook)
Library of Congress Control Number: 2025931191

Cover by John Yates / www.stealworks.com
Interior design by briandesign

10 9 8 7 6 5 4 3 2 1

PM Press
PO Box 23912
Oakland, CA 94623
www.pmpress.org

Printed in the USA.

CONTENTS

PREFACE

On 25 June 1975, Donald Oliver Soper, the Right Honourable Lord Soper no less, a Methodist minister, committed socialist, and active participant in the Campaign for Nuclear Disarmament, stood in the House of Lords—an institution which he questioned the very existence of—to ask the government what progress had been made regarding the review of homelessness announced the previous year. "In 1969, applications for temporary accommodation,' he asserted 'made by homeless families to local councils in England and Wales numbered 22,000, an intolerable number. When the last available figures came to hand—that is, in 1973— the number had risen to 33,000." With 1,249 families in 1974 in temporary bed-and-breakfast accommodation and in 1972 an estimated 1,415 people sleeping rough in Central London, this was a matter of significant horror for Soper.[1]

In the United Kingdom today, fifty years of progress means there are now an estimated 350,000 homeless, more than 180,000 of them in London, including twelve thousand rough sleepers documented on the streets of the capital in 2023–2024. This is a testament to a city where more than a billion pounds' worth of property is owned by money launderers actively facilitated by the legal and financial services sectors, where 7.8 percent of housing stock is vacant including 47,000 second homes, the average monthly rent is £2,000 and an average home is £567,000.[2] Ideas such as the belief that commerce and the state must act for the good of citizens, that humanity has a higher calling than business, and that we all bear a responsibility for our fellow citizens, seem to have receded, that is if they were ever influential to begin with.

The past is a strange river. It doesn't do to romanticise it unduly, but it's still fascinating to imagine a London where an entire school could be unofficially occupied from 1975 to 1983, providing accommodation for those in need and those wishing to devote themselves to music, acting as a political centre and a creative arts venue, providing a backdrop for filmmaking, photography, poetry, performance art, and activism. For many years, I'd known the name 'Centro Iberico,' the abandoned school on Harrow Road, but it existed in my mind only as an unreal phantasm, void of history. Which school? Who squatted it? How did the anarchists find it? What went on there? When did it close?

What mainstream culture does very well is archiving: any event or object deemed significant is reproduced across media formats and proliferated in a never-ending cycle of anniversaries and special occasions. The underground lacks the infrastructure for such extensive capture and duplication, meaning a significant percentage of grassroots activity winds up merely as footnotes to superstar stories or vague remembrances from those who were there. The hundred words dedicated to Throbbing Gristle's gig at Centro Iberico in Simon Ford's *Wreckers of Civilisation: The Story of COUM Transmissions & Throbbing Gristle* was likely the first time I heard the name, otherwise it was a hollow title glimpsed occasionally in a gigography or release credit.[3]

More than twenty years later, working on a volume regarding the indefinable yet glorious entity that is The New Blockaders, their main instigator, Richard Rupenus, became the catalyst for this book in late 2022. He was insistent that he performed at the venue with his brother Philip, but couldn't confirm when or tell me anything else about it — the hunt for more information and confirmed dates began. Soon, I was obsessed by it.

As recently as December 2024, the Wikipedia entry for Centro Iberico consisted of just eight sentences, three of them merely listing band names.[4] Online sources were scattered, piecemeal, providing brief and often contradictory glimpses of the space. Soon I was engrossed in the blotchy print type of back issues of *Sounds* magazine on microfilms in the British Library; delving into the local London press at the British Newspaper Archive website; receiving kind hospitality from the City of Westminster Archives; reading a decade and a half of the anarchist newspapers *Black Flag* and *Freedom* thanks to The Sparrows' Nest Library and Archive, a Nottingham-based volunteer group preserving the history of British radicalism; and spending dozens of hours with individuals kind enough to gift me their minds and memories. While wildly distracted from the book I was meant to be writing, I was possessed by a determined desire to tell Centro Iberico's story before finite human lifespans, limited documentation and broken links silenced all memory of it.

The resulting story is one of strange connection and of new lives arising after rupture or cataclysm. It's a tale of a recently exiled Spanish Civil War veteran and his new life with Britain's homegrown anarchists; of the Angry Brigade and the abuse of power known as the Persons Unknown trial; of a Victorian school house and a squatters group linked to The Clash; of no love lost between aging anarchists and young punks, despite their temporary alignment around Wapping's Autonomy Centre; of a name denoting a peripatetic circle funding anti-Franco activities that was then bequeathed to Spanish squatters forging a mixed space for politics and culture with a future super-producer living on the school grounds; of the hard grind of Kill Your Pet Puppy and Scum Collective in a final feverish year of activity that ended with the inevitable demolition notice.

While working, I was consistently inspired by how little an individual needs, materially speaking, to forge something of worth in this world, that a driving belief held in our mind about what we create having value, is a formidable defence against self-doubt, despair, or the subjugating force of external disapproval. I found that inspiration, whether in the pages of Miguel J.M. García García's memoir, *Franco's Prisoner*, which attests to a lifelong devotion to his cause; in many conversations with Tony Drayton, whose intellectual curiosity and generous nature were consistently energising whenever my own will flagged; or in the company of Mark Wilson of The Mob, while being shown around

Rockaway Park—a physical testament to kindness, community, and the ongoing existence of free spaces.

My fondest hope is that the existence of this work will reinvigorate the name 'Centro Iberico,' drawing together the available information and providing a clarity and fresh understanding. I also hope it will encourage further information to surface as I'm sure there is more to tell. Even today, while writing this foreword, I realised that it was Lord Soper himself who gave permission for Miguel J.M. García García to begin his new organisation at the Parish Hall of Holy Trinity, Kingsway; he was standing in for the Anglican vicar when he chose to give García's vision a home.[5] It's true we are all connected wherever we stand in society's eyes, we are always one.

ACKNOWLEDGMENTS

Thank you to the individuals who permitted their photographs to appear as part of this work, namely: Chris Low, Eduardo Niebla, Erica Echinberg, Kevin Thorne, Mickey Penguin, Laurie Mayer, Mark Wilson, Michael Baxter, Mick Slaughter, Paul May, Philip Ruff, Richard Rupenus, Steve Pegrum and the Angels in Exile Records Archive, and William Orbit. Thanks also to the Sparrow's Nest, the City of Westminster Archives, the British Library, the Conway Library at the Courtauld Institute of Art, to Derek Walmsley and the team at *The Wire* magazine, and to Max Smiles and Jacksons Lane.

A further profusion of thanks are owed to people who I interviewed for this book, or connected me with others, or pointed me in the right direction—I hope you will accept the existence of this work as a thank you dedicated to all of you.

Finally, there's a thank you owed to Karima Abbaci for being patient while I rave about places and people she's never heard of or dance a jig of delight over a blurry scan of a 1982 gig listing. If I replaced every piece of paper in every archive in the world, with notes saying 'I love you,' I'd still need more paper because it wouldn't be anywhere near enough notes.

BORN OF STRUGGLE, LIVING IN HOPE

A man of lesser will might have quit a dozen times, but Miguel J.M. García García was a fighter. Growing up in a family committed to the Spanish anarchist movement, he had seen his father—an organiser with the Confederación Nacional del Trabajo (CNT)[1]—tortured by the police to the point that he could no longer work, soon succumbing to the flu epidemic of 1920. At age eleven, García became the man of the house working to support his family.

Barely a year later, García joined a strike by newspaper boys and took part in street protests. Faced with young boys refusing to work and complaints from newspaper proprietors, the local division of Spain's paramilitary gendarmerie, the Guardia Civil, reacted with an armed cavalry charge leaving two teenage protesters dead and an officer wounded in the eye from a stone thrown by García. His mother arranged the flight of her twelve-year-old revolutionary to safety in France. A life of peace could have beckoned, instead, García gave his energies to anarchism and thus began a decade-and-a-half political apprenticeship lived on both sides of the border.

At the outbreak of the Spanish Civil War, García drove guns across the Pyrenees to aid the CNT-FAI militias, joining them to fend off the attempted Fascist coup in Barcelona in July 1936.[2] Seeing thirty-two months of combat on two fronts, his only pause was due to a bullet through the leg, which simply meant a brief hospital stay of around a week after which, while leaning on a stick, he stepped in as a trainer for student volunteers with whom he returned to the front line.

Despite such exertions, the republic collapsed in 1939 and the Fascists unleashed a triumphal vengeance in which tens of thousands died, while hundreds of thousands fled the country. A less ardent believer in anarchist principles might have joined them in flight when the battlefront collapsed.[3] Instead, García was swept up on 9 May into a makeshift and barely sanitary camp in the Pueblo Nuevo district of Madrid, then despatched to the Miguel De Unamuno concentration camp. Perhaps a man possessing less tenacity might have been cowed by twenty-two months of 're-education.' García, on the other hand, immediately encountered the gradually organising resistance against the newly installed dictator, Francisco Franco, and spent the Second World War smuggling Jews out of Nazi-occupied France. He learned new skills as a forger courtesy of MI9, the British Directorate of Military Intelligence responsible for aiding the escape of Allied personnel from Axis territory, including the route across the Pyrenees.

In the aftermath of the war, García worked with the Tallion Group, a unit of the anti-Franco resistance, quietly rebuilding the anarchist union movement in Spain in the face of continued hostility from the authorities. On 21 October 1949, his time as a free man came to an end and he was arrested with several comrades. The courts moved slowly. It was 7 February 1952 before García, alongside ten colleagues, was sentenced to death. A month later, on 13 March, his sentence was commuted to life imprisonment. And, the following morning, five of his codefendants were marched out of Madrid's Carabanchel Prison to the 'campo de la bota' (boot camp), a remote spot on a nearby beach where, in peacetime, children had been taught to swim. A firing squad formed five times, loaded five times, fired five times.

García's story could have ended here, a tale lost to time, soon to become one more forgotten body buried behind prison walls, a man unmourned by a world more interested in package holidays and the potential for sunbathing on the dictatorship's blood-soaked sands.

FREEDOM

Approaching Christmas 1968, hunger strikes by Spanish political prisoners aroused considerable sympathy, leading to an easing of restrictions on their ability to communicate with supporters nationally and internationally. This prompted the arrival of petitions from legal conferences and well-connected organisations abroad, a swelling wave of care packages: attention that annoyed the regime almost as much as the prisoners' acts of passive resistance. The government's animosity, however, was moving on from old wars and defeated warriors to focus on ETA's paramilitary campaign for Basque independence.[1]

Amid these changing times, after twenty years and thirty hours in captivity, García was released on 22 October 1969. With no life to return to, in a Spain he didn't recognise, he soon made enquiries regarding travel abroad and was invited to apply for a passport. On the understanding that he could never return—but where in the world to go?

A few years earlier, in Madrid's Carabanchel Prison, García had encountered Stuart Christie. Christie was a Scottish anarchist who had been arrested in Madrid on 11 August 1964 while smuggling explosives for use in an assassination plot against Franco.[2] Only eighteen, Christie served three years before being freed as an act of clemency, supposedly in response to a plea from Christie's mother, but primarily in service of Franco's desire to quell opposition from abroad through such gestures. Heading to London, he was received by Albert Meltzer who had been a key figure in the campaign for his release. Meltzer was a veteran of anarchist causes: as a young man, he had organised the smuggling of

18 years in Franco jail

To the slogan 'There are no political prisoners in Spain' it may be retorted, 'There are still political prisoners who have served more than eighteen continuous years'.

Miguel Garcia Garcia—now in Soria—60 years of age, militant of the CNT, is now the 'father' of the Spanish prisons. He was detained in Barcelona on October 21, 1949 —the same date as Juan Busque Bergés, who was judged by court-martial in the Military Headquarters of that city in February 1952 and condemned to death (being commuted at the last moment, on March 13 of the same year, with three others). Another five were shot in the Campo de la Bota, Barcelona, after the same court-martial.

Now Miguel Garcia Garcia, half-blind and critically ill, is still languishing in the prison of Soria, hoping against hope that the authorities will allow him to die outside prison.

Lately he has been suffering severe heart attacks and was saved only by a miracle—he was taken to Yserias, where he remained two months during which period he saw no heart specialist. The crisis over, he was returned to Soria at 1,100 metres altitude, where a new crisis would of necessity be fatal.

It is imperative that something be done very soon on behalf of Miguel Garcia Garcia. He cannot be left to die among the warders of Soria, a latter-day victim of the Spanish Inquisition.

STUART CHRISTIE

Christie on García (*Direct Action* 9, no. 2, February 1968)

Meltzer and Christie, Conway Hall, 1976 (Courtesy of Phil Ruff)

weaponry to the CNT-FAI militias during the Civil War; worked for the Spanish anarchists' short-lived intelligence service; contributed to various anarchist periodicals while taking an active part in a range of strikes and other causes; and founded Wooden Shoe Press, an anarchist printer.

Christie acted on his recent experiences by founding the Anarchist Black Cross, reviving the name of a group that had aided revolutionary prisoners in Tzarist Russia, to send aid to Spanish prisoners. Meltzer, having merged his Anarcho-Syndicalist Committee with another group to form the Black Flag—who also published a journal of the same name—proceeded to fold his organisation into Christie's with the two of them now publishing *The Bulletin of the Anarchist Black Cross*, ultimately renamed *Black Flag* in January 1971. In February 1968's edition of the newspaper, *Direct Action*, Christie lobbied for García's release, making claims that García was half-blind, a recent victim of several heart attacks, whose only desire was "to die outside prison."[3] The aging anarchist would become a key cause pursued by the Anarchist Black Cross and García was persuaded to join its instigators in London.

Now a man of sixty one, an age where many are contemplating retirement, García would renew his struggle. Meltzer, then employed as a copytaker at the *Daily Telegraph*, found work for García in the printworks for *The Times*. Stable accommodation was secured when two Spanish students, one of whom was conveniently called García, arranged to move home to Spain. They agreed to let García Senior take over the lease on their flat at 123 Upper Tollington Park with the landlord none the wiser. While he had exaggerated García's ill health in his 1968 article, Christie did have to arrange medical care for his new associate because the shock of release paralysed muscles in his throat leaving him barely able to speak. Support was provided at a clinic on the continent via Octavio Alberola, an anarchist comrade under house arrest in Belgium.

Portrait photo of Miguel García at Centro Iberico (1976)

The London Committee has now decided that in future Miguel Garcia Garcia - who has now secured asylum in this country - will act as International Secretary; Stuart Christie will be Defence Secretary; and Albert Meltzer will act as Correspondence Secretary and edit the bulletin.

The Spanish exile movement in London - Movimiento Libertario - has now set up a PRISONERS COMMITTEE and we will co-operate with them in support of prisoners in Spain. Aid on behalf of those in Franco's jails may go either direct, to us, or to the "Comite pro Presos".

ON THE 20th JUNE there will be a concert at the CONWAY HALL held by the Pro-Presos Committee organised by 'Mujeres Libres'.

_____

The Black Cross is operating the SPANISH LIBERATION FUND to subsidise the activist groups in Spain. Money received will be sent direct to aid the resistance groups and will not be accounted for. Resistance activities are entering a new phase of vital struggle when every blow counts and the Liberation Movement needs every penny it can get without having its hands tied.
For this reason, we are keeping this aspect of our support quite separate from the matter of aid for prisoners.

Establishing positions in the summer (*Black Cross* 1, no. 8, June 1970)

SPAIN NOW—
AND NEXT?

Meeting Organised by
ANARCHIST
BLACK CROSS

at 'FREEDOM' HALL,
84b Whitechapel High St., E.1
SUNDAY, FEBRUARY 15,
at 8.30 p.m.

Speakers:
Miguel Garcia Garcia
(Just out after 20 years in jail)
Stuart Christie
Chair: Albert Meltzer

Miguel García's first speech in London (*Freedom* 31, no. 5, 14 February 1970)

SECOND LIVES

At the Freedom Press Hall, Whitechapel, on Sunday 15 February 1970, García stood before a packed room of sixty to seventy attendees and, in fluent English picked up from English-speaking prisoners, began his testimony.[1] While his voice was still so frail that Christie sometimes had to repeat his statements so the audience could hear, García drew the crowd in with his hard-earned knowledge of what fighting for a cause truly meant. The talk covered the Spanish resistance movement post-1939 up to the present day, the plight of Franco's political prisoners, and then opened up to discussion on the needs of the present moment in Spain.

Following this success, the June issue of the Bulletin clarified his role in the Anarchist Black Cross: "Miguel García García— who has secured asylum in this country—will act as International Secretary; Stuart Christie will be Defence Secretary; and Albert Meltzer will act as Correspondence Secretary and edit the bulletin."[2] His confidence buoyed by the warm reception in February and the encouragement of his friends, he spoke at Conway Hall next before embarking on a speaking tour of the UK, then extending his talks to Italy and Germany.

This was not just dry academic reflection on events hundreds of miles, or even many decades, from the reality of London at the dawn of the 1970s. A backdrop of left-wing violence aimed at national governments elsewhere in Western Europe had been stoking police suspicion of the British left, as well as inspiring individuals wishing to go beyond pickets and protest marches. García, who was steeped in experience of the oppressive role

García in 123 Upper Tollington Park (Courtesy of Phil Ruff)

García at home with a Spanish trade union comrade (April 1979)

García attending the Concert for the Forgotten Veterans (3 April 1976)

of law enforcement in Spain, was now comrades with Christie, who had been under police observation since his return to the UK; and with Meltzer, who had fought police escorts defending a Fascist march as far back as the famed Battle of Cable Street in October 1936.[3]

Amid an atmosphere fertile with revolutionary zeal, attacks credited to the 1st of May Group, a Spanish anti-Franco resistance unit, had taken place in London as far back as August 1967. This was nothing, however, compared to the scale of activity from May 1970 onward. Christie credits García's first speech as the direct inspiration leading to the formation of mainland Britain's only homegrown postwar terrorist group: the Angry Brigade. Four individuals who saw García speak—John Barker, Hilary Creek, Jim Greenfield, and Anna Mendelson—were arrested in a police raid on their shared house at 359 Amhurst Road, Hackney, on 21 August 1971. Christie and Christopher Bott were arrested that same day while visiting the address in question. The arrests continued with Angie Weir (11 November), Chris Allen (17 November), Pauline Conroy (26 November), and Kate McLean (18 December).

While Conroy and Allen would be released due to lack of evidence, the others were put on trial as the 'Stoke Newington Eight' from 30 May to 6 December 1972 with the prosecution claiming they were responsible for twenty-seven bombings and shootings, the first on 22 May 1970.[4] At the end of the trial, only the original four arrestees were found guilty, each sentenced to fifteen years reduced to ten due to the jury asking the judge for clemency. Given the timing and Christie's proximity to the events in question, there's little reason to doubt his claim that, faced with García—someone who had truly fought for anarchism and been willing to pay the price—individuals within the audience had chosen to fight.[5]

FINDING COMMUNITY

Amid his early speaking engagements in spring 1970, García had been persuaded to write a brief pamphlet on his experiences entitled *Looking Back … After 20 Years in Jail*.[1] He soon began work expanding it into what would become a full book, *Franco's Prisoner*, published in 1972. In May 1971, meanwhile, an announcement appeared in *Black Flag*, for whom he was a regular contributor. It was a simple statement: "The Centro Iberico (Iberian Centre) is holding meetings each Sunday at 5.30 at the Parish Hall of Holy Trinity, Kingsway."[2]

García inherited the name from a Spanish Communist collective whom he encountered in the process of vacating both name and premises and who would reopen elsewhere as either the Garcia Lorca Club or the Club Antonio Machado. London possessed a strong Spanish community with Portobello Road at its heart, particularly on the stretch from Garcia's Deli (no relation) at no. 248 to the Galicia restaurant at 323—the CNT's international offices had been located there and had provided logistical support to those fleeing in the aftermath of the Civil War. Many families in London had ties to the anarchist militias and were happy to have a new social hub. The Anarchist Black Cross had already developed ties with the Spanish exile movement, the Movimiento Libertario, having agreed in 1970 to cooperate on fundraising with its *Comite pro Presos* (Prisoners Committee).

One survivor of that era, Eliseu Huertas Cos, personally experienced the ties between the British and Spanish scenes.

Eliseu Huertas: My aunt Maria had married a Welsh ex-miner who worked in the British Embassy in Madrid and he had been responsible for taking Stuart Christie to the airport to be extradited. I had to leave Spain in 1968 to avoid being drafted into the army. I lived in Bath where, through the countercultural press, I discovered there was a Spanish underground in exile after reading a review in *Oz* of García's book *Franco's Prisoner*. In the climate of the time, it felt like the only options left for the counterculture were conformity, infiltration to change things from within, or terrorism. Moving to London in 1974, I met a lady handing out Communist Party leaflets and visited the Club Antonio Machado which, alongside Centro Iberico, was where the Spanish resistance was at work. I tied myself to them and over the next two years travelled to Moscow, then to Romania—remember it was forbidden under the dictatorship for anyone to do so. We were militants but could at least act without being murdered though we were aware we were under surveillance from within our ranks. It was around that time that I first met García in person. I remember mentioning where my family was from in Girona and he knew that one of his comrades, Quico Sabaté had been ambushed in the area; he had also met Manolo Sabaté in prison before his execution.[3]

With Meltzer providing funding, Centro Iberico soon became a hotbed of activity funnelling support to the new generation of activists in Spain; gathering donations via the Spanish Liberation Fund run by the Anarchist Black Cross; accepting clothing donations to either be sent to Spain or resold to raise cash; pressuring Spanish ministries and embassies with letter-writing campaigns and direct protest; rescuing Spanish girls who had arrived in the UK as 'au pairs' only to find themselves used as domestic slaves; as well as helping women requiring abortions due to Catholic Spain's strict attitude toward contraception. The first known event staged at the centre was a lecture on Sunday 9 May by Professor A. García

Spanish movement will also
be giving lectures in May.
On 9th May (Sun. 5.30) at
Iberian Centre, Prof. A.
Garcia Calvo, Professor at
Madrid expelled for supporting the student revolt, will
speak on "The University -
New Forms of Power and New
Forms of Revolt".   The
following Sunday 16th May
(Sun. 5.30 same place) the
meeting will be addressed
by Jose Peirats, on the
situation in Spain. Peirats
is the most important historian of the C.N.T.   BOTH
THESE LECTURES HOWEVER WILL
BE IN SPANISH.   Questions
in English can be answered
(in Spanish) for those who
understand the language but
cannot speak it well.

─────────────────────

The Centro Iberico (Iberian
Centre) is holding meetings
each Sunday at 5.30 at
the Parish Hall of Holy
Trinity, Kingsway (directly
opposite HOLBORN TUBE
station).   Those who do
not speak Spanish are
invited to come along about
8. or 8.30 and mix socially
as this is the nucleus of
an international centre.
At present it is trying to
integrate exiles and
immigrant workers from
Spain but we have hopes it
will develop into a
libertarian international
centre.   Refreshments
available.

─────────────────────

Announcement of Centro Iberico's opening (*Black Flag* II, no. 5, May 1971)

MEETINGS

Nearly 2200 people jammed into the small parish hall to hear José Peirats lecture (in Spanish). The libertarian was well represented (some 150 or so of those present) ranging from exiles of thirty years – and their children and grandchildren – to immigrant workers and students, visitors on a temporary basis and new exiles. The rest of the 200 included some communist critics.

Peirat's success (*Black Flag* II, no. 6, June 1971)

Looking back...
after 20 years in jail

Looking Back ... After 20 Years in Jail by
Miguel García (pamphlet, 1970)

FRANCO'S
PRISONER
MIGUEL GARCIA

Franco's Prisoner by Miguel García
(Granada Publishing, 1972)

Church of the Holy Trinity, Kingsway (Belcher & Joass, CON_B04248_
F001_014/Courtesy of The Conway Library/Courtauld Institute of Art,
cc-by-nc)

season.
The International Libertarian Centre – apart from being the one social meeting place of anarchists in London – has played a valuable
part in building the movement in Spain and Portugal by Centro Iberico meetings building contacts in the peninsula, and by the
organised lessons in offset printing – as well as "sidelines" like finding jobs and places to stay for many who had to leave suddenly
(plus organising hospitality for girl students coming here for abortions). The joint fund for prisoners and resistance has been
extremely valuable in several countries. A good sale of these posters at the present-giving season will give us a boost on both.
(The second in the series will be 'Sabate' – the third 'Zapata'.)

Activities of the International Libertarian Centre (*Black Flag* III, no. 15, November 1973)

Calvo, a professor expelled from Madrid University for support-ing student revolts. This was followed on 16 May by a talk from Jose Peirats, an expert on the CNT. Both lectures were in Spanish though, as a concession, questions could be asked in English and answers would be translated.[4]

García's ambition was twofold: first, Centro Iberico was a social and political hub for the Spanish community in London. Second, from the start he invited non–Spanish speakers to join the meetings for what would become the Centro Internacional Libertario (International Libertarian Centre) aimed specifically at the anarchist community. The centre would maintain links with organisations and individuals abroad, acting as a clearing house for information that would then be shared via the anarchist press. In addition, joint meetings were held with the Anarchist Black Cross to encourage and expand local London-based polit-ical engagement.

Stability, however, was hard to find for these fledgling insti-tutions of British anarchism. Meltzer, who had moved in with García at 123 Upper Tollington Park, was not paying rent on the *Black Flag* offices at 10 Gilbert Place, squatting at the premises until a private detective agency moved in in 1973. Friends of Meltzer's, Ted Kavanagh and Lyn Hudelist, came to the rescue.[5]

A few years earlier, with partial funding from Meltzer, Kavanagh and his former partner, Anna Blume, had run the Wooden Shoe anarchist bookshop on Old Compton Street. When forced to close, Kavanagh and his new partner, Lyn Hudelist, needed somewhere they could install their printing press and settled on a basement at 83a Haverstock Hill, between Chalk Farm and Belsize Park. Originally rented by the greengrocer above to a religious group, the latter had held firm to their desire for spiritual purity and scarpered when the greengrocer was replaced by a bookmaker. The space was then used for band rehearsals until the anarchists—far less squeamish about proximity to worldly sins—moved in.

Both Black Flag and Christie's publishing imprint, Cienfuegos Press, would declare the basement its new headquarters in June

1973. That same month the announcement went out: "Centro Iberico, which is no longer holding its meetings in Holborn, will also resume in the same premises, for which we are now negotiating." Meetings paused for several months before Centro Iberico moved into the new location in late summer.[6]

ANARCHY ESTABLISHED
... AND DISESTABLISHED

No longer sharing space in the church, meetings at Centro Iberico expanded to both Saturdays and Sundays, then 4:00–8:00 p.m. on weekdays too from autumn 1975. Anarchist Black Cross member, Philip Ruff, guides us through the premises:

> **Philip Ruff**: When you opened the front door there was a small room to the left.... To the right, a steep flight of stairs dropped down to the basement premises.... At the bottom was a large room.... Parallel to the stairs, abutting the meeting room, was a smaller room which housed an offset printing press.... Between the print room and the stairs was a short passage leading to a small kitchen.... The kitchen opened out on one side to a tiny courtyard and outside toilet. The wall opposite the courtyard was used to display anarchist papers and a few books. At the far end of the room was a low counter, behind which sat Miguel García and a gas cooker, on which Miguel would whip up delicious paella.[1]

The earliest known talk in the basement was the North London Organised Revolutionary Anarchists' public meeting on 'Revolutionary Anarchists in the Class Struggle' on Thursday 23 August 1973. Education was a key purpose of the centre: for example, a series of 'Solidarity Seminars' under the banner of the Centro Internacional Libertario on Saturdays in mid-1975—17 May ('New Struggles in Society'), 31 May ('Anarchism in Britain'), 14 June ('Socialism and Self-Management'), and 28 June ('The Economy.')[2]

The basement also became a space for entertainment, such as the anarchist cabaret that took place each weekend in February 1974.[3] There would also be a regular cycle of films: April–May 1974 saw showings of Luis Buñuel's *Nazarín* and *Viridiana*. With the Anarchist Black Cross, Centro Iberico would support the staging of larger festivities at Conway Hall such as the *Grand May Day Gala* on 3 May 1975 or the concert on 3 April 1976 for 'forgotten veterans of the Spanish Civil War,' namely disabled Republican soldiers deprived of pensions. Donations flowed through Centro Iberico to the Anarchist Black Cross; anarchist publications were sold and distributed; and its other community-focused and political activities ramped up once again.

The death of Franco in November 1975 was a lightning bolt electrifying all those who hoped for Spain to escape the long shadow of dictatorship. In the early days of 'la Transición,' many anarchists still languished in prison but progress came swiftly. By mid-1977 *Black Flag* declared: "All the long-term libertarian prisoners in Spain are now released." García poured his still-substantial energies into the rejuvenation of the CNT, acquiring printing presses and duplicators for the union so they could evade the censorious mainstream press and put forth their independent positions to the public. The newspaper, *ZERO*, declared in June 1977: "Anyone who can assist in any way, either by donating a duplicator or contributing financially, should contact Miguel García, 123 Upper Tollington, London N4. Clearly mark all letters CNT."

The excitement of this moment—the end of dictatorship; the resurrection of the union to which García and his family had been devoted—was rather disrupted by events in the summer of 1976. The bookmaker landlord of the Haverstock Hill basement paid an unannounced visit and was rather annoyed to find a guest of the Anarchist Black Cross living in the space, one John Olday, an elderly artist and lifelong activist.[4] In his autobiography, Meltzer lays the blame for the eviction squarely on Olday saying that he had been complaining to the landlord about rats, thus alerting the landlord to his presence and to the fairly extensive space under his feet.

The anarchists were duly ordered to vacate the premises with September's issue of *Black Flag* announcing the permanent closure of Haverstock Hill: the landlord proceeded to turn the space into a gambling den. While the date of the visit is unknown, the final event reported was a commemoration of the death of Bakunin on 1 July with fifty individuals in attendance and no mention of trouble. The anarchists' departure took place amid the following eight to ten weeks.[5]

The September editorial in *Black Flag* does hint that the landlord's inspection was not entirely unprompted. The writer of the piece, likely Meltzer himself, grumbled about "revolutionary tourists from the continent wanting a holiday on the cheap," "rising costs" and "the total absence of contributions." This focus on money might indicate that the anarchists attempted a repeat of their trick from 10 Gilbert Place and had stopped paying rent only to be called on the manoeuvre far more promptly by their current landlord.

Either way, the anarchists were now scattered. Still enduring significant police harassment in the long aftermath of the Angry Brigade trial, Christie had been advised to leave London, heading first to Yorkshire around May 1975, then moving to the Orkney Islands early in 1976. While still edited in London under the stewardship of Meltzer and a rota of editors, *Black Flag* began using Christie's home in Sanday as its official address while, for a time, 123 Upper Tollington Park became the mailing address for the Anarchist Black Cross.

By November 1976 Centro Iberico was meeting in "the converted church directly opposite Highgate Tube," a former Wesleyan Methodist property opened in 1905 and converted into a community arts centre after its closure in 1975.[6] The initial announcement mentioned "Centro Iberico/Int. Libertarian Centre now meeting every Sunday at 5–11pm," This was quite a step backward from the freedom of Chalk Farm and during its time at Archway, any gatherings were sufficiently low key to be lost to time.

Communications to:
BLACK FLAG,

83a Haverstock Hill,
N. W. 3.

CHANGE OF ADDRESS.

Eating out once a month? The
Chalk Farm & Belsize Dinner is to
be started early in June. The
name will commemorate a tradition
of anarchist publishing and activity in Chalk Farm and Belsize Road
and in fact we will be holding the
dinners in that part of London.

Subscription is £1 per dinner
and this includes good food and
wine.   Nosh will be preceded by
gab, and any profits will go to
the Black X or any cause of the
moment.   We contemplate holding
the dinners once a week (probably
Saturday at 10 p.m) and hope all
sympathisers in or visiting the
London area will be able to make
it at least once a month.

Details will be sent (when
ready) to anyone who writes in,
and also be available in next
month's issue.

The Centro Iberico, which
is no longer holding its meetings
in Holborn, will also resume in
the same premises, for which we
are now negotiating.

Centro Iberico moves to Camden
(*Black Flag* III, no. 3, June 1973)

PUBLIC MEETINGS

"*ORGANIZED*
REVOLUTIONARY ANARCHISTS
IN THE CLASS STRUGGLE"

8 P.M. WEDNESDAY 22 AUGUST
THE CLARION CLUB
89, PARK HILL S.W.4.

8 P.M. THURSDAY 23 AUGUST
CENTRO IBERICO
83A HAVERSTOCK HILL N.W.3.

NORTH LONDON ORA

**Anarchist meeting at
Haverstock Hill (flyer,
August 1973)**

García in the kitchen at Chalk Farm (Courtesy of Phil Ruff)

* ANARCHIST CINEMA
Saturday 27th & Sunday 28th of APRIL.

NAZARIN by Luis Bunuel (Mexico 1958 - Spanish
dialogue - English sub-titles.)

Saturday 4th & Sunday 5th of MAY.

PRAISE MARX AND PASS THE AMMUNITION by
Maurice Hatton (U.K. 1969).

Saturday 11th & Sunday 12th of MAY.

VIRIDIANA by Luis Bunuel (Spain/Mexico 1961 —
Spanish dialogue - English sub-titles).

At CENTRO IBERICO at 7.30.PM
••••••••••••••••••••••••••
83A Haverstock Hill, London NW.3. – side entrance by
Steele's Road - tube Chalk Farm/Belsize Park - Buses 31
& 68 (Chalk Farm stop).

**Anarchist Cinema at Centro Iberico
(*Black Flag* III, no. 10, 1974)**

**ALL CORRESPONDENCE TO BLACK FLAG,
83a, Haverstock Hill, London N.W.3, tel:- 586 2038.**

In support of political prisoners ANARCHIST CABARET
February 2th and 16th; Cabaret of the Minorities "Gai
Chansons" February 9th and 23rd. All performances at
83a, Haverstock Hill, Start 8 p.m. SHARP. Doors open
7.30. p.m. International Libertarian Centre - Centre Iberico
will meet in future only on Sundays, 7 p.m. All welcome.

Anarchist Cabaret,
February 1974 (*Black Flag* III,
no. 8, January 1974)

Anarchist publishing: García's pamphlet on the Spanish resistance (c. 1974–1977)

London School of Economics "teach-in" by the Libertarian Iberia Committee, with Philip Sansom and Albert Meltzer (8 May 1976)

* A further £10 in tickets was also due but not received by the date of balancing. We realise we probably "cut our own throat" financially by asking for support for prisoners and resistance causes, as a result of which our appeal to keep the paper going suffers, but do your best friends. Once we sell enough literature we won't need to ask for cash, and "all good stuff, no rubbish" (see columns). Our London centre is the contact base for international activity and merits a lot more support than it gets. Also remember we can do with a lot of things besides cash: e.g. trading stamps will help us; we need clean rags for printshop and always have a demand for scrapmetal which we can sell for one or other causes, likewise records, clothes etc for jumble use.

Because many of our readers are sending money direct to prisoners in various countires, and we never know who is, we are always reluctant to stop sending the paper to anyone whose sub has lapsed — but as a result we send the paper (with an added waste in postage) to addresses — the dead, the moved, the lapsed, the lost . . . if you ever do any of these things bar the first let us know, so we can take you off the mailing list.

Grand May Day Gala at the CONWAY HALL, Sat. May 3

The Grand May Day Gala at Conway Hall (*Black Flag* III, no. 19, April 1975)

BAKUNIN
COMMEMORATIONS

THE CENTENARY of Bakunin's death in Berne on 1 July 1876 was celebrated in London at two separate occasions. On the previous weekend, a disco was held at the Roebuck pub, arranged by the Federation of London Anarchist Groups, to raise funds for anarchist causes.

On the centenary day itself, about fifty people attended an informal meeting at the Centro Iberico to remember Bakunin's contribution to the anarchist movement and to discuss his relevance a hundred years later. The chair was taken by Wynford Hicks, and the opening speakers were Nick Heath, Albert Meltzer, Nicolas Walter, and José Martin-Artajo.

Informally chatting about Bakunin (*Freedom* 37, no. 14, 10 July 1976)

Sat. 17th January "La Comunidad del Sur" (Community of the South), a talk ill. with slides, by a spokesman from the S. American anarchist movement on 'An experience of the libertarian way of life where everything was brought into question - work, leisure, sexuality, education.' At Centro Iberico, 83a Haverstock Hill, NW3 (entrance in Steele's Rd). Tube: Chalk Farm or Belsize Park. Starts 7.30 p.m.

Anarchist talks at Centro Iberico (*Freedom* 37, no. 1, 10 January 1976)

THE FORGOTTEN VETERANS

A concert in aid of the disabled and war-wounded of the Spanish Civil War in exile who receive financial support neither from the Spanish nor British Governments and who are left dependent upon charity for their 'crime' of fighting for liberty in Spain against Franco's fascism.

Those artists giving their time and talents in order to focus public attention on these forgotten veterans include:

JOHN WILLIAMS   *internationally famous classical guitarist*
CARLOS BONELL   *Spanish guitarist extraordinaire*
VIRAM JASANI   *sitar player with tabla accompaniment*
'COKAYGNE'   *Birmingham based folk group*

SATURDAY 3 APRIL, at the Conway Hall, Red Lion Square, London WC1. £1. starts 7.30pm; Buffet and Bookstall open 7pm.

Organised by the Organisation of Spanish Civil War Wounded and the Spanish ex-Combatants Association. All money raised in aid of those wounded, crippled or mutilated in the Spanish Civil War. Further details from Centro Iberico, 83a Haverstock Hill, London NW3.

Anarchist fundraising for the "forgotten veterans" (3 April 1976)

García visiting the Plaça de Sant Felip Neri where many of his comrades were killed (1979)

PLEASE NOTE THAT OUR ADDRESS is now c/o Cienfuegos Press, Box A, Over the Water, Sanday, Orkney Islands.
Our London centre at 83a Haverstock Hill, London N.W.3., is now permanently closed. We hope to open a new London centre soon. As sporadic letters still get sent to 10 Gilbert Place, and are lost, we hope that the occasional letters and persistent libertarian newspapers that never revise their addresses will take heed that "83a" has passed us and now houses a swish gambling club unlikely to be interested. Letters for the Centro Iberico can be sent to Miguel Garcia, 123 Upper Tollington Park, London N.4.

LONDON CENTRE: There is supposed to be a libertarian presence in London other than ourselves. Maybe it ought to emerge a bit more noticeably than it has done. For four years we have borne the expense and problems of a "centre" without any support providing not only a meeting place but an international centre. Rising costs beyond any hope of meeting them, with the total absence of contributions towards the upkeep, have forced us to give up the International Libertarian Centre.
    Ideally such a centre demands far wider support than that of one or two people, who are already fully occupied with other matters — and on whom descend like locusts "revolutionary tourists" from the Continent wanting a "holiday on the cheap" which to say the least, is discouraging.

Centro Iberico/Int. Libertarian Centre now meeting every Sunday at 5-11pm at Community Centre, Archway Rd., London N 19 (converted church directly opposite Highgate Tube).   For libertarian contact and social meeting

Announcement of the move to Jacksons Lane (*Black Flag* IV, no. 11, November 1976)

Closure of Haverstock Hill (*Black Flag* IV, no. 10, September 1976)

ZERO

No.1 June 77. 20p.

Anarchist/Anarca-feminist Monthly

Spain: March 27 '77: bullring San Sebastian de los Reyes

Spanish Anarchists Reorganise

On Sunday March 27th, the anarchist National Confederation of Labour (CNT), the largest trade union in Spain until the arrival of Franco's fascist regime, held its first public meeting since the civil war. About 30,000 people packed the bullring in San Sebastian de los Reyes, 10 miles outside Madrid. Most of those present came from Madrid and the surrounding areas, which in the past has never been a stronghold of the CNT

The meeting began late as loudspeakers announced "the main road is blocked, and we're expecting the whole of Europe to arrive". The crowd were emotional and euphoric. A few people chanting "Spain tomorrow will be republican" were drowned out by the chants of "Spain tomorrow will be Libertarian", followed by "the people united manage without parties" and "fascists, bourgeois there are only a few months left". There was a minute's silence for the victims of the repression, followed by speakers including regional delegates, a representative of the International Workers Association (AIT), and the national secretary of the CNT, Gomez Cases, who started the meeting with the declaration that "the CNT is the only organisation which guarantees the autonomy of the workers. All comrades have the same status, there are no leaders in the CNT."

The vertical trade unions, including the Communist Party controlled Workers Commissions, were the target of much anger, "nauseous and evil-smelling corpse of a crumbling capitalism." Before the meeting broke-up, a collection for the CNT raised about 200,000 pesetas, and messages of greetings and solidarity were read out from the I.W.W. in Chicago, the Bulgarian anarchist movement in exile,

comrades in Hong Kong, Black Cross and Centro Iberico in Britain and many others. The CNT had organised its own stewards for the meeting, and the police and Guardia Civil made no appearance.

In the weeks following this meeting, many others of CNT locals took place, including the construction syndicates in Madrid who print their own paper Construccion, CNT theatrical workers, and a CNT section in the multi-national I.T.T. Every province in Spain now has a regional CNT federation, with a network of local and district federations. Libertarian and CNT papers are rapidly starting up. In Barcelona, Solidaridad Obrera has a growing circulation of over 10,000, and in Madrid a national CNT paper has produced 2 issues.

The return of the CNT has coincided with the flourishing of a strong counter-culture movement amongst young people in Spain. Publications with emphasis on sexual freedom, rock music and drugs, but at the same time consciously anarchist, are appearing. The Spanish Communist Party (PCE) and other left groups have been making statements that the CNT is today a movement of homosexuals and hippies. It is. It is also a movement of workers, peasants, feminists, students, conscientious objectors, in fact all those who suffer oppression at the hands of authority and the state. The old CNT militants, veterans of the civil war and countless other struggles still make up a small percentage of the membership, but the strength of the CNT today, lies with the young workers and students, who were not even born when the war ended. Ninety per cent of the current membership are young people, with an average age of around 30.

Unlike the PCE (and countless others), the CNT has made no compromises with

the Suarez Government, but says instead it will stick to the time-honoured working class path towards the social revolution. Near the end of April, the principle trade unions were given permission to apply for legalization (part of the liberal facade), the CNT was the only union which refused to co-operate. The same day the applications for legality were handed in, a ban on all May Day demonstrations was announced by Suarez. The demonstrations which went ahead were ruthlessly attacked by the riot police and cavalry. Hundreds of people, adults and children, demonstrators and bystanders were injured, many seriously. So much for liberalism.

The elections being held on June 15th will be as predictable as they are corrupt and contrived. Over 150 parties have put up candidates — so far — ranging from socialists to fascists, monarchists and Carlists to separatists. The CNT will be taking no part in this circus, and can only benefit from the petty party squabbling which will no doubt be in plentiful supply.

The left parties participating in the elections, especially the PCE, are falling over themselves to show how moderate they are, and how they all believe in the cherished ideal of social democracy. The PCE has already done its best to prevent grass-roots actions from developing, and has been actively discouraging strikes and militancy by its members. The fascists and right wing in Spain are still extremely powerful. The dismantling last month of Franco's political machine, the National Movement, was merely cosmetics, attempting to provide a liberal image which is needed if Spain is to be accepted in the E.E.C. The leadership of the armed forces, the paramilitaries and the police is still solidly Francoist, (the Franco Lives brigade, even though the old bastard has

been lying in his personally designed mausoleum for 18 months), and they have made it known they are unhappy at the present course of events. The economy is depressed, unemployment is rising, and living standards falling. The need for an independent working class movement, the CNT, dedicated to fight for the interests and demands of the workers becomes obvious.

Although the recent events have been greatly encouraging they have only been small steps towards the reconstruction of the CNT and anarchist movement in Spain. Comrades in Spain will decide for themselves what course events will take, but the libertarian movement worldwide can offer practical support and solidarity. Whilst support for the communist and socialist controlled unions comes in from labour organisations abroad, the CNT receives only small contributions, i.e. — The International Libertarian Labor Fund recently sent $1,000 directly to the CNT in Madrid. The press outside Spain lie, distort and in most cases refuse to recognise the fact that a Spanish libertarian movement exists. Money is desperately needed to finance propaganda activities. The Black Cross in London, (an anarchist prisoners-aid group) has been sending out old or unused duplicators and presses to different locals of the CNT. This is one practical, immediate way we can help. Anyone who can assist in any way, either by donating a duplicator or contributing financially, should contact Miguel Garcia, 123 Upper Tollington, London N4. Clearly mark all letters CNT.

The first issue of the national CNT paper printed in December 1976, had a cartoon bearing the slogan, "courage grandparents, we are coming" signed CNT.

The anarchist movement in Spain has once again resurfaced ☐ Pete Webb.

ZERO 1 June 77 Page 1

Anarchy for Spain (*Zero no. 1, June 1977*)

Opening party for Jacksons Lane, 1975
(Courtesy of Jacksons Lane)

Main nave at Jacksons Lane, 1980
(Courtesy of Jacksons Lane)

Exterior of Jacksons Lane during a road widening protest, 1983
(Courtesy of Jacksons Lane)

NO POINT IN ASKING

Amid this moment of great change for Spain and for Centro Iberico, Britain was shaken by its own cultural earthquake: punk.

The Sex Pistols had been gigging since November 1975 with nary a whisper of political intent. Their songs mostly boiled down to era-typical teenage kicks against parents, teachers, and vaguely rendered authority figures. The song that would change that, 'Anarchy in the UK,' was debuted live on 20 July 1976, performed for Granada Television's *So It Goes* in September, then released as the band's first single on 26 November.... All without sparking revolution or inevitable counterrevolution. Interviewed for the *London Weekend Show* on 28 November, Britain's newest pop enfant terrible, John Lydon, made clear that his song was not targeting the institutional power structure; his enemies were music fans in their twenties and thirties: "complacent, apathetic old fucks who … watch *Top of the Pops* and send their boring little letters into *Melody Maker*, week after week. That's what I wanna get rid of."

His flippant use of 'anarchy' took on a life of its own amid the media hysteria that followed the Sex Pistols' 1 December appearance on Bill Grundy's show *Today*. Earlier in his career, Malcolm McLaren, promoter and manager for the Sex Pistols, had attempted to spark interest in the New York Dolls by dressing them as Communists, a move that failed as no one could mistake the famously louche Dolls for activists. With the Sex Pistols' offering far more combustible tinder, McLaren reheated the marketing move by dangling revolutionary chic from the chorus of the Pistols' best-known song. The Pistols suddenly, but not so mysteriously, began touting anarchy as their creed.

With one record ("Anarchy in the U.K.") and a small amount of pissing and televised swearing, the Sex Pistols punk-rock band burst into the British press in a big way. To the papers they are Anarchists, plain and simple. Our comrades Noel and Marie Murray, though, whilst awaiting their appeal on Dublin's death row, were "anarchists" – with inverted commas, and "self-styled" ones as that! The Sex Pistols conform to the Fleet Street view of what anarchism is of course – wild-eyed and vomiting, spreading outrage and vandalism. Anarchism as a revolutionary creed is dismissed or left to gentle academics for dissection. When in doubt reach for inverted commas, or better still substitute "Marxist" or "nationalists!"

Still for all Fleet Street's calculated ignorance, what about the Sex Pistols? Does their brand of punk-anarchism bear a second startled look? Not as anarchist propaganda it is sure; but then it is only music (or noise, or theatre). "You pays your money, and you takes your choice." Need we expect more? Some clearly do, though perhaps it would be more fruitful for the anarchist movement if they expected more of themselves. One after the other, half a dozen "self-styled" comrades, impress on me how punks like the Sex Pistols and their like are giving anarchism a bad name. Could it be worse already? Apparently so. Johnny Rotten has succeeded where Winston Churchill failed; *les Enrages* are out-raged! Yet if punk-rock IS getting anarchism a bad name it is certainly getting the crowds too; whilst the anarchists with ruffled feathers, who assure this is the case, certainly are not, for all their righteousness.

Punk bands are chastised for paving the way for fascist hordes because a few of their number sport Nazi emblems (next to pictures of Karl Marx) and have

LISTEN PUNKS!

a passion for leather gear. If fascism did seize power the punks and their young working class fans, who revel in the ridiculous and violent, would be marked down for early entry into concentration camps. Authoritarians of any brand can not tolerate the outspoken. Trendy pacifist liberals who snigger at the Sex Pistols but raise Bob Dylan to King should laugh while they can. If fascism does engulf Britain the advantage of shooting at pacifists is that they don't shoot back. But the street punks, like every generation of working class youth before them, are not so tame. The dumb insolence and aggression bred into them at school or in the dole queue is fertile ground for resistance. It may be that they will be future storm troopers

but it needn't be. It is not the Sex Pistols who are to blame if every teenager doesn't become a revolutionary. If the National Front are attracting disillusioned Labour voters from the working class it

would be more useful to think why WE are not attracting them.

The same people who hailed Mick Jagger as an "anarchist" in the 60s and now wax hot under the collar over a few punks having fun ought to ask themselves a few questions. Mr. Jagger is not the "street fighting man" he used to be, but then he never was. Perhaps Johnny Rotten will climb the same ladder to tax-evading seclusion as part of the musical establishment too. That is not the point. People can listen to what music they like. The Sex Pistols, or any musician will not inspire the unemployed to revolt, but then we shouldn't need them to. It is not the punks who give anarchism a bad name, it is too many people who are anarchists in name only.   **Henry Black**.

"Listen Punks!" (*Black Flag* IV, no. 13, February 1977).

The London *Evening News* carried a feature on the "Swastika Revolution" linking the Sex Pistols ("Anarchy in the UK") and their fans with the National Front. Full of the sinister quasi-political insinuations that are ostensibly establishment liberal and in fact designed to boost the NF among working class youth.

There was a reply from their manager: "ANARCHY
I would like to point out that the Sex Pistols are not into any political party, least of all the loathsome National Front, mentioned by John Blake in the Swastika Revolution.

We and our fans, do not and will not co-operate or associate with the National Front.

Anarchy is not fascism but self-rule and a belief in following ones own way of life without recourse to dictatorship or nationalism. We hate this kind of army nonsense.
M. McLaren, Manager Sex Pistols, Oxford Street, W.1."

Their music may be as rotten as they say it is but what they are saying sounds as melodic as Beethoven.

Hitting the note of rebellion may nowadays hit the jackpot in the music scene — though we had to smile ruefully at the Melody Maker's headline "There's money in Anarchy" (for what we've picked up plus the proverbial ten cents you could get a cup of coffee) — and the pressure on the kids ultimately to conform will be great. But the punks are no punks in getting anarchy over to some of the kids in the working class where it belongs.

Getting anarchy over to some of the kids (*Black Flag* IV, no. 15, 1977)

Our concert at the Conway Hall was very badly attended (possibly due to snow in the suburbs) — but thanks especially to Robbie and Sandra who worked like beavers to raise the cash out of the audience, we broke even with a small benefit for the Mutual Aid Project. However we have decided to make the disco a monthly event. No charge for admission (but we'll ask for a donation to whatever our current cause is, Black Flag, Mutual Aid, Black Cross, prisoner defence or whatever). Obviously we need a meeting place for Black Flag readers and a social get-together where we can arrange other meetings is the best idea we can think of.
FRIDAY 12th MAY
Start around 7 or 8. Conway Hall, Red Lion Square, London WC.1. (nearest tube, Holborn).

Anarchist disco (*Black Flag* V, no. 4, May 1978)

Traditional anarchists were irked that the press swallowed the Pistols' claims based on cliches about what anarchists supposedly looked like: "wild-eyed and vomiting, spreading outrage and vandalism."[1] They were also tepid toward the punks co-opting the anarchist 'A' without much sense of its meaning. On the other hand, some circles warmed to how effective these ragged children were at communicating with the British working classes, certainly far more effective than the anarchists themselves had been. In the spring, *Black Flag* was positively chirpy as it reported on a spat between the *London Evening News* and McLaren, who refuted the newspaper's suggestion of a Pistols association with the National Front by declaring his wards' allegiance to anarchy as "self-rule and a belief in following one's own way of life."[2]

Even as the Pistols' press-confected threat to public order was being comprehensively defanged, tossing the word 'anarchy' into the waters of youth culture caused ripples. Communism in the UK had been tainted by apologetics for Stalin and whataboutery when faced with the authoritarianism of the Soviet Union. The subsequent grouping of ideologies gathered under the 'New Left' banner then lost momentum in the late 1960s as the state developed new tactics to contain their protests. Many activists became demoralised by the institutionalised routine of march, protest, petition—no progress. The new generation sought less hierarchical, less predictable, less staid means of rebellion whether this meant Situationist-inspired antics; rebellion as a lived experience in the form of squatter or traveller lifestyles; a focus on single causes such as animal rights or nuclear disarmament. The challenge was that punk's typically British anti-intellectual and ahistorical attitude, combined with the limited horizons of youth, meant its participants believed they represented a Year Zero, a new generation with no future and no past either. This was not an audience reading Bakunin or reading up on the Spanish Civil War.

Shaking off the past allowed for a redefinition of what anarchism could mean. Up-and-coming groups like Crass declared themselves anarchists to opt out of the traditional left-right division of British politics with its obligations in terms of messaging and interpretation. While not an ideology in and of itself, punk anarchism provided a banner of convenience under which a wide array of causes could gather for open-minded support.

The Anarchist Black Cross, while believing punk to be just another popular capitalist fashion trend, did notice the shift in youth culture. The organisation staged a punk concert at Conway Hall in the spring of 1978 and reported that, while the event had not necessarily met high hopes for attendance, it was sufficiently successful that they would inaugurate a monthly free disco to share information, seek fresh-faced participants, and request donations to worthy causes.

NEW MOVES

In contrast to all this teenage lightning, in 1977 García was a sixty-nine-year-old man who, although sprightly considering the travails of his life, was shrugging off bouts of ill health. In 1976 he had visited Spain which whetted his appetite to return home a free man. While he continued to reside at Upper Tollington Park until sometime in 1978, arrangements commenced for a permanent move to Barcelona. Supporters who knew how much he had given for the cause set him up with a café bar in a former blacksmith's shop: La Fragua (The Forge).

García's departure was representative of a wider generational shift as the fortieth anniversary of the republic's fall loomed. Those among London's expat Spanish community with a direct tie to the anarchist militias or resistance to Franco were now aging, dying, or joining García in returning to their newly democratised country. With the Spanish Civil War increasingly a matter for historians, new causes such as Germany's Red Army Faction or Northern Ireland's paramilitaries, increasingly occupied the spotlight among Britain's anarchist 'establishment.'

Against this backdrop, the year and a half spent sharing space at the Jacksons Lane Arts Centre ended. The anarchist newspaper *Freedom* announced on 26 November 1977: "Centro Iberico now meeting at 421a Harrow Road, London, W9. Saturdays and Sundays 3–11pm."[1] The notice confirmed that García continued to be the venue's contact point and that the other aspect of the centre's activities would continue with "Internat. Libertarian Centre mtgs soon."

Harrow Road, running parallel to the Grand Union Canal, was a long parade of shops catering to a predominantly working-class

London
—

CENTRO IBERICO now meeting at 421 Harrow Road, London W.9. Saturdays & Sundays
3-11 pm. (Postal address: Miguel Garcia,
123 Upper Tollington Park, London N.4.
(Internat. Libertarian Centre mtgs soon.

Announcement of Centro Iberico's Move to Harrow Road (*Freedom* 38,
no. 23, 26 November 1977)

CENTRO IBERICO
address: 421 Harrow Road, London W9.
(near Portobello Road: Tube Westbourne
Park).
Saturdays & Sundays: 3 - 11 p.m.
(POST: Miguel Garcia, 123 Upper
Tollington Park, London N.4).

Black Flag confirms the move (*Black Flag* V, no. 2, 1977)

Playground of the North Paddington Lower School, c. 1955 (Courtesy of City of
Westminster Archives)

population in the adjacent residential streets. These included furniture stores, stalls out in the street at weekends, fruit and veg, old warehouses, small merchants, and a registry office. Amongst these workaday surroundings, the final home of Centro Iberico stood out: a late nineteenth-century school building on three floors. Letters from mid-December 1882 show the commissioning of Stimpson & Co. Builders of 78 Brompton Road "for the erection of New Board School ... on the canal side of Harrow Road adjoining Eastwoods Wharf." The result was the North Paddington Lower School which opened in 1884—the Upper School was on nearby Amberley Road.[2]

The urgency of its construction was due to the area's massive population growth—from 46,306 in 1851 to 107,000 by 1886—combined with its dearth of educational facilities: in 1853, the Paddington area possessed only four schools, catering for 666 boys and 449 girls in total. Classes were taught to infants on the ground floor, girls on the first, and boys on the top floor. The school leaving age was just eleven for the school's first years of operation, rising to twelve in 1899, fourteen in 1918, fifteen in 1947, which made the site increasingly cramped and unsustainable.

By the mid-1950s, the school was merged into the wider North Paddington Secondary School and began hosting adult education classes in the evenings as the Paddington Junior Commercial and Technical College, the latter then changing name to become the Paddington College for Further Education, further adding to the profusion of pseudonyms for this establishment. Closure came in the summer of 1973 with the building of a new comprehensive and amalgamation with other local schools. From then on, the building was used as an education guidance centre and, during school holidays, to host youth clubs the last of which departed in September 1975.

At some point that year, the council commissioned several photographers to create a documentary record of Westminster. One photographer, Melanie Louise Simo, walked the Paddington area and was clearly struck by the imposing bulk and beauty of the old school. Reproduced here, Simo took the premises from

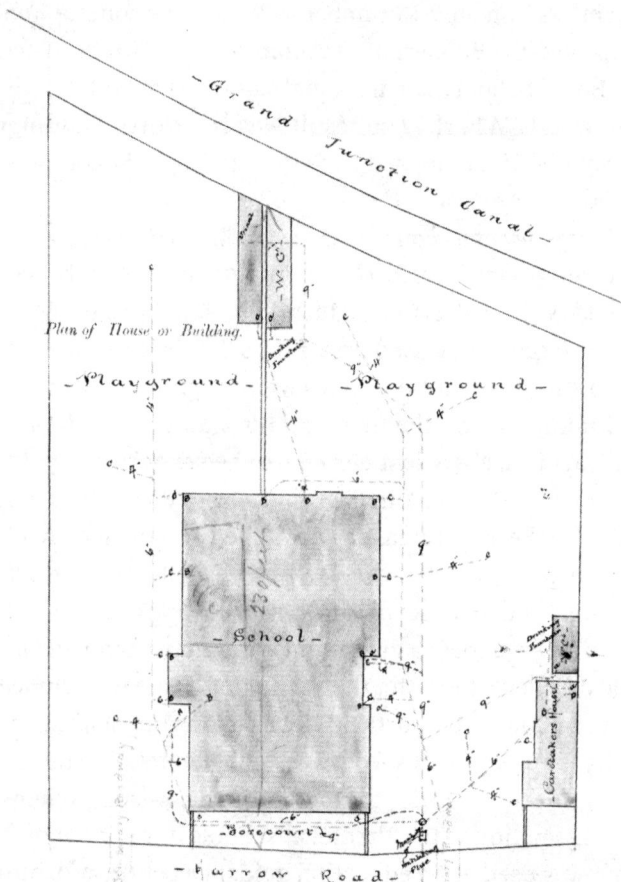

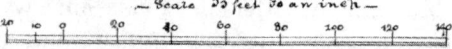

Hand-drawn plan of the future school, 1882 (Courtesy of City of Westminster Archives)

three angles: from Portnall Road looking across Harrow Road; from a few paces further west along Harrow Road itself, her image encompassing the entire frontage overlooking the playground; then a final shot looking backward from Bravington Road. Mostly intact windows testify to the recency of the school's closure. Unfortunately, in October, the now-empty school was raided by vandals who broke in causing significant damage and looting whatever remained of value including lead from the roof.

The scale of dereliction coupled with the council's desire to sell the site meant there was no enthusiasm for the significant costs of repair. At that point, an organisation headquartered just up the road at 19 Elgin Avenue stepped in: the Maida Hill Squatters. The group, having celebrated its second anniversary back in June, were running several properties, and possessed the experience and connections to set up a successful squat. They occupied the school in the week beginning Monday 3 November declaring their intention to protect the building and to make it available for use, setting up a committee to handle discussions and inquiries of that nature.

This change in occupation likely explains how local musicians became involved. Richard Williams of The Derelicts performed at a benefit gig there sometime in late 1975–early 1976 alongside the 101ers.[3] Both bands were in nearby squats: the 101ers were barely five minutes up the road at 101 Walterton Road (the Maida Hill Squatters helped Joe Strummer and his compatriots into the property) while Williams was in Latimer Road, a thirty-minute walk away. The 'Diary of Live Gigs and Recording Sessions' for The 101ers included in Richard Dudanski's *Squat City Rocks* memoir contains a tantalising 'venue unknown' date on 21 December 1975 for the "Maida Hill Squatters Party" which could very well be this first event at the school.

Richard Williams (The Derelicts): I only remember it as 'the squatted school' and don't remember who the benefit was for…. It was definitely downstairs but I can't remember if there was a stage, I suspect not. We would have dragged

View from across Harrow Road, 1956 (Courtesy of City of Westminster Archives)

LONDON COUNTY COUNCIL
PADDINGTON JUNIOR COMMERCIAL
AND TECHNICAL COLLEGE
(PRINCIPAL : FRANK PITT, M.A.)
NORTH PADDINGTON SECONDAY SCHOOL,
421A HARROW ROAD, W.9. (LAD 4607)

HAVERSTOCK SCHOOL, CHALK FARM, N.W.3.
ST. MARYLEBONE C. OF E. SCHOOL, 64 HIGH STREET, W.1.
ACLAND SCHOOL, FORTESS ROAD, N.W.5.
REGENTS PARK SECONDARY SCHOOL, CAPLAND STREET, N.W.8.
CARDINAL MANNING SCHOOL, ST. CHARLES Sq., W.10.

EVENING COURSES are provided at a small fee for Students from 15 years of age.
COMMERCIAL COURSES include Gregg and Pitman Shorthand, Typewriting, Commerce and English.
TECHNICAL COURSES incluce Mechanical and Electrical Engineering Carpentry, Technical Drawing, Calculations and Science.
GENERAL COURSES include Mathematics, English, Chemistry, Physics, Biology, English for Students from abroad at Belsize Branch, Haverstock School, Cambridge Lower and Proficiency Certificate.
EXAMINATIONS. Students are prepared for many public examinations: General Certificate of Education, Royal Society of Arts and College of Preceptors. In addition there is a Preliminary Course for the City and Guilds and National Certificates.
ENROLMENT begins on September 21st, 1959. Details of fees and further information from the Principal at the College. (1611)

Evening classes and adult education at Harrow Road (*Kensington News & West London Times*, 18 September 1959)

our own PA and backline in as we did at all our gigs in those days. I remember chatting to Joe (Strummer)—or Woody as he was known at the time—about our band van: a long-wheelbase Transit with aeroplane seats! He was very impressed with it as the 101ers were driving around in an ancient hearse!

Squatting the premises was not an exceptional choice at the time. On 1 December 1968, the London Squatters Campaign occupied a block of luxury flats providing inspiration to a broad swathe of people in unstable or undesirable accommodation; rough sleepers in dire need of shelter; those stuck on interminable council housing waiting lists; the thousands in bed and breakfasts or hostels; as well as idealistic seekers of a life beyond mainstream society.

Lea Nicholson: I was touring so paying rent all year wasn't an option, meaning I got involved in squats on Crogsland Road in Chalk Farm from summer '72. There was a distinct tie-in between people squatting, people running bands, people making music, people making films. There was a big house around the corner on Prince of Wales Road, which had a huge yard where they'd set up a stage for bands to play, a guy called 'Doctor John' was a kind of informal leader there. Three or four houses were squatted on Crogsland Road: No. 5 was squatted by people involved in the Angry Brigade, one of them was out on appeal; I was at No. 11; then there was Sid Rawle who was a guiding light behind what became the New Age Travellers.

When we moved out of that squat we spent several weeks in the house of an architect. A friend, a journalist for the *Morning Star*, lived in a basement flat in a huge house off Haverstock Hill which had been divided into bedsits—presumably someone owned it but for whatever reason it had fallen empty. She said to me, "Why don't you squat upstairs?" She provided the key and we moved into

THE headmaster of Paddington's new comprehensive school is already hard at work preparing for its opening next September.

He is 51-years-old New Zealander Mr. Norman Thomson, who has been teaching in secondary school, in Britain since 1957.

The new comprehensive will be formed by the amalgamation of Paddington and Maida Vale High School for Girls, in Elgin Avenue, and North Paddington School.

The High School's existing premises will be retained. New £490,000 buildings, standing in six acres of grounds, are nearing completion in Oakington Road.

Mr. Thomson, married with two children, has taught at Aylestone School, Willesden Green, and was headmaster of Churchmead Secondary School at Datchet, Buckinghamshire.

Asked whether introducing the girls to a mixed school was likely to create problems he told our reporter: "I think the problems are in the minds of the parents, rather than the children. Children are not quite so sheltered as their parents are inclined to believe."

He went on: "As I talk to the girls, I find that they are looking forward to the amalgamation, and children from both schools are excited by the wider educational opportunities that will be available. My main preoccupation is to make sure that the teachers they get are of the highest calibre."

There is already an impressive team of 40 men and women on the staff, and more are being appointed. Number of pupils in the new school next September will probably be between 1,050 and 1,100—of whom 150 will be sixth formers.

"I think there is a certain social justice about the comprehensive system," said Mr. Thomson, "and the size of the school gives you resources which aren't available in smaller communities."

The Paddington area has a diversity of communities, and Mr. Thomson believes that respect for importance to pupils of having the opportunity to work to the limits of their ability. The curriculum the individuality of each pupil—regardless of background or ability—and the social relationships established in the school will help to create cohesion. Prizes and credit will be given for effort and character, as well as for purely academic work.

Mr. Thomson stresses the importance of parental involvement in children's education. "The parents' attitude to education and their understanding of what the school is doing are of great significance for the children's progress," he says.

Already he has initiated meetings at which parents can come and ask him questions, and he has made himself available for personal interviews. He intends to continue this process of information and consultation through information sheets and brochures, open days and meetings. "A school should not see itself as cut off from the community, but as providing a specialised service for the family," he says.

On the academic side, he stresses the need for standards. The curriculum will cover some 14 subjects, grouped to encourage an "inter-disciplinary" approach. Academic "high-fliers" will be encouraged to diversify beyond their own specialist subjects and undertake some less academic work.

"There will be emphasis on raising standards of speech, reading and writing, because of the importance of self-expression," in English to every young person."

The main teaching block is the new Oakington Road complex consists of science laboratories and rooms for housecraft, needlework, art and pottery, metal and woodwork, as well as a general classroom. A smaller building, linked by a covered way, includes a large activities hall, a gymnasium and rooms for drama, music and music practice.

Mr. Thomson intends to base the first three years on the new buildings, with the next three years using the old High School premises. "There will obviously be a certain amount of overlapping," he says, "and I am determined that we shall not be split into Upper and Lower schools. I aim to promote a sharing of educational experience."

North Paddington Lower School in Harrow Road. The Inner London Education Authority plan to dispose of the site and offers are being invited from developers. Right:

School closure (*Marylebone Mercury*, 23 February 1973)

From Portnall Road, 1975 (Melanie Louise Simo, courtesy of City of Westminster Archives)

this huge place, fifteen to twenty bedsits, then it turned out this Irish guy was already squatting there. He'd been in for months on his own and nobody had known! It was a weird old scene. People doing things as part of a mutual support movement, then people acting in isolation, ferreting away underneath the whole thing.

'Punk squats' would become common, giving refuge to young punks who arrived in London either fleeing home life or running toward a new life they could believe in.

Steve Ignorant (Crass): A lot of punks moved into squats when they got old enough to leave home but, if they could, they'd set up their own 'punk squats' rather than moving into one of the established ones. People tend to forget though that the original squatting organisations gave them a lot of help, quite a lot of the established squats had set up their own community centres and advice centres and things like that by this point, so there was a strong affiliation.

Andi Sex Gang (Sex Gang Children): I spent two years in my late teens in Abercrombie Street, Battersea. I was staying with friends in West Kensington and there was a record store and this guy said there was a very organised group down in Battersea: the Battersea Squatters Association. He took me across there and I remember seeing on the lampposts, black-and-white fliers with 'Wanted Dead Or Alive' and a picture of the local chief of police from Battersea Bridge police station—I thought, 'I like these guys' style!' The police in Battersea were notorious for beating people up and people had died in their custody. They'd do it in the black and whites, just beat the shit out of them so the council estates and council blocks could see it.

This was '78, right in the middle of enemy territory, people who hated squatters and threatened to burn us out.

The school from across Harrow Road, 1975 (Melanie Louise Simo, courtesy of City of Westminster Archives)

Looking back from Bravington Road, 1975 (Melanie Louise Simo, courtesy of City of Westminster Archives)

For us, it was about fighting for rights, especially for single people who were bottom of the ladder. The private housing and renting laws were abominable. We were involved in helping people who wanted to start unions in the restaurants but were getting intimidated by the owners; and we'd help people who were homeless, battered housewives, and people like that. We were involved in anti-Nazi stuff too, we'd go into East London and stand guard outside Asian stores that were getting petrol bombed. I remember this old couple, he'd fought in World War Two and didn't like 'squat types' but his wife told him to ask for help. It was the middle of winter and their gas was going to be cut off. We just said, "Don't worry, we'll sort it out," and we did. I won't go into detail about what we did but it was good to help those people.

Kay Byatt (Youth in Asia): Everyone was squatting, nearly everyone I knew! You'd find empty places and move on in, it was so easy it meant there were squats opening up all over. People would help each other out: there'd be someone who knew how to connect the electric, how to get the water back on, how to change the locks, people who knew all the rules and regulations.

By the end of the 1970s, an estimated fifty thousand squatters nationwide had turned disused buildings into viable homes. The majority were based in London due to the availability of tens of thousands of abandoned properties emptied for (usually long-delayed) redevelopment, as well as the mutual assistance of the squatting community. Negotiating to move Centro Iberico into an old classroom at weekends was a fair financial decision in a cash-strapped anarchist scene.

It isn't clear when the former school acquired its Spanish character, nor how García came to learn of it. It is understandable, however, why the presence of a Spanish contingent professing an allegiance to anarchism would lead to an encounter.

Caretaker squat at Harrow Road school building

SQUATTERS have taken over a disused Paddington school in a bid to bar vandals from the building.

And they have set up an ad-hoc committee to represent all community groups and interested parties who may want to use the building.

Vandals have caused considerable damage at the old North Paddington Lower School, Harrow Road, over the past three weeks.

Windows have been smashed, taps turned on and lead stolen from the roof.

At first, youth and community leaders were on the point of giving up hope of bringing the building into use.

Area youth officer Mr. D. E. Cox was negotiating to use the school as an evening centre for the Paddington Churches' Youth Association.

Mr. Cox said the building had been rendered "quite unsuitable for use."

But Maida Hill Squatters had other ideas.

They occupied the school last week, and one squatter has been staying in the caretaker's cottage at night to make sure nobody enters and causes further damage.

Squatters' leaders are now trying to galvanise community groups to renew their interest in using the building, which has been empty for two years.

Spokesman Mr. Alan Davis said: "We took over the school to prevent further vandalism.

"We would like the school to be used by the original groups who were campaigning for it to remain open."

The Inner London Education Authority, who own the building, are planning to demolish it.

Architect Mr. Colin Bex said the building could be brought into use but probably at a cost of about £3,000.

The ILEA say they will not consider repairing the building. A spokesman said they had been trying to dispose of it for some time.

Mr. Bex, who is supporting the squatter's action, said there was an urgent need for more community facilities in the area, particularly for children.

He said the building could still be adapted for that purpose.

Community relations officer Mr. Malcolm Lawrence said he had asked Paddington's G.L.C. councillor Mrs. Jean Morriton, and G.L.C. deputy leader Illtyd Harrington to take some action over the school's future.

"The G.L.C.'s incredible bureaucratic rule book has delayed a decision on the future of the building," he said.

"All we are asking is for them to take some positive decisions. The result of their inactivity is a completely vandalised building."

Since the closure of the school in 1973, the building has been used as a day-time education guidance centre and, during Christmas and summer holidays, as a youth club.

But the last youth group left the building in September—and the wreckers moved in.

FOR TRIAL

ACCUSED of dishonestly using electricity at his home in Elgin Avenue, Maida Vale, Nathan Friday (34), packer, was at Marylebone Court committed for trial at the Crown Court, Knightsbridge.

delay a £120,000 "open space" scheme any further.

The plan includes a toddlers' play area, old people's garden and an adventure playground.

The scheme is planned for a three-acre site in Ilbert Street, between Fourth Avenue and Third Avenue.

Miss Masey told the council's town planning committee that the nearly finished showpiece Mozart Estate had been vandalised by youngsters with nothing to do, and the proposed play scheme could

● Guarded by squatters . . . the old North Paddington School building in Harrow Road.

A "caretaker squat" at the Harrow Road School
(*Marylebone Mercury*, 14 November 1975)

Eliseu Huertas Cos: Someone at the Machado knew about Centro Iberico and I met García again at Harrow Road. At that stage it wasn't a music venue, it was very much a part of the political resistance. This changed rapidly as social democracy took hold in Spain. Amnesty meant direct resistance dissipated and Centro Iberico lost its clandestine glory and its political appeal as the old-timers returned home. After that, it mutated and became an active cultural squat, a refuge for musicians, but one with historical resonance for underground culture.

To this point, Centro Iberico existed as an organisation held together by García's will, following him between locations, and focused specifically on a Spanish cause that had essentially come to an end. From here on, Centro Iberico ceased to be associated with any single individual and was bound inextricably to one location: 421a Harrow Road. As early as October 1978, gig posters already referred to the entire location as Centro Iberico. It's a mark of the respect felt for García and for the history of the institution that the residents of the school adopted the name, wrote it several feet high on the outer wall, and retained it until the end of their days at the site.

NO FUTURE / A FUTURE

It was inevitable that Centro Iberico would change after García's departure. It was he who had been the international touring speaker; the regular contributor to *Black Flag*; the prime instigator of the centre's significant span of social, political, and humanitarian activity. The intention to renew meetings of the Centro Internacional Libertario never came to fruition, so the flow of information to and from a continent-wide network of comrades ceased.

Political activity did continue, perhaps reflecting his presence in 1978. There was a 26 March performance of the works of poet Miguel Hernandez, who had died in a Fascist camp in 1942; a rush-produced leaflet publicising the murder of Agustín Rueda by guards at Carabanchel Prison; and a public meeting for Anarchist Day on 11 November. The latter included an 'Anglo-Spanish social' continuing attempts to connect local supporters with the Spanish community.[1]

Anarchist press coverage became ever more limited as Centro Iberico shed its former life and became a creative arts venue. *Black Flag* and *Freedom* were selective in publicising upcoming events, defending a clear line between pure entertainment versus political activity worthy of their attention. Punk's generational shift and reforging of anarchism as a popular cause twisted 'anarchy' into shapes only loosely tied to the concept that the tiny circle of politically dedicated predecessors espoused, making both sides dismissive of one another.

Steve Lake (Zounds): I used to live in a cooperative with a few people who were running the Rising Free bookshop on Upper Street in Islington—Sisterwrite, the feminist bookshop, used to be there too. The older sort of anarchist centred around Freedom Press thought we were these out-of-control kids and that we had anarchy symbols because it was the equivalent of having a fast motorbike. "These kids haven't read Kropotkin. They've not read Bakunin ..." And they were right! But there wasn't much nurturing or loving about it. They were very dry and theoretical. It got a lot more interesting when *Class War* came along: they didn't care much about the theory and they just wanted to bash the rich which, again, isn't my position either, but still!

It was a fairly typical manifestation of the disdain generations reaching parental age often hold for the new ideas of the young, spiked with the added rigidity of civil religiosity, the commitment to ideological and textual rectitude over openness.

Penny Rimbaud (Crass): I'd been through it before with the hippy thing, the free festival thing, all the schisms and arguments. None of the brotherhood of compassion essential to anarchism because, without fellowship and ... not empathy but true compassion, it can't operate.

The popularisation of 'anarchy' also served to dilute the attention that could be paid to any single organisation. Contact pages in the anarchist press now listed numerous groups even just within London: the Libertarian Communist Group, Anarchist Communist Association, Direct Action Movement, Anarchist Feminists, Anarchy Collective, Freedom Collective, East London Libertarians, Hackney Anarchists, Kingston Anarchists, West London Anarchists, and others. These groups were as likely to argue with one another as they were to ally against common foes as Ignorant explains: "There were so many schisms: you had anarcho-syndicalists, anarcho-feminists, anarcho-situationists.... All of them disagreeing! Crass were getting stick from all of them because we weren't coming up to their expectations or doing what

JOE HILL MEMORIAL.

October 7th will be the hundredth anniversary of the birth of Joe Hill, the famous I.W.W.organiser.He is chiefly remembered for his political songs which were popular with working people throughout North America between the wars. The Industrial Workers of the World attempted to encourage all waged workers to organise one great revolutionary Union.They were brutally suppressed due to their massive influence.

Joe Hill was framed on a murder charge and shot by firing squad.In his last letter he said 'don't mourn,..organise.' In his honour,we are organising a day-long commemoration.(In this we are joined with other syndicalists and libertarians). SAT OCT 6th — all night party,with music,beer and maybe food.Kids room. 9pm on.

At Centro Iberico,the school,42Ia Harrow Rd,W9.(Westbourne Pk).£I...(50p unwaged) SUN OCT7th.- Speakers corner I2-4pm,speaking,heckling etc! Mass meetings again! 5-IO.30 films and discussion,at Action Space,Chenies St,WCI.Bring your friends....

Left parties and unions serve only the interests of corporate capital, not the interests of the workers. There will be no more wage rises under capitalism, no matter who is in power. The only way forward is to form our own autonomous workers' organisations and fight for the socialisation of industry - in other words, for the Social Revolution.

Ned Ludd.

Joe Hill anniversary (*London Workers' Group Bulletin* no. 6, 1979)

Over a hundred people attended the presentation of the work of Miguel Hernandez on March 26, organised by the Aula de Literatura of the Ateneo Libertario (Centro Iberico) in London. (Given in Spanish). The young libertarians associated with the Centro Iberico also rushed out a leaflet on the murder in a Spanish jail of Agustin Rueda, especially calling attention to the abuse of language in the Spanish press — headlines stating soberly "Ten prison functionaries responsible for the death of a prisoner in Carabanchel" contrasting with "Vile murder of the director of prisons."

Anarchism marches on at Centro Iberico (*Black Flag* V, no. 4, May 1978)

ANARCHIST DAY – NOVEMBER 11

Friday and Saturday Nov 10 & 11; Anarchist stall (Cienfuegos & Black Flag) at the Socialist Bookfair,St. Pancras Town Hall.

Evening, Saturday 11, Centro Iberico, 420 Harrow Road, London W11. Public meeting 7.30 p.m. followed by joint Anglo-Spanish social.

Anarchist Day 1978 (*Black Flag* V, no. 6, October 1978)

4 FREEDOM

ANARCHIST-FEMINISM – WHERE DO WE GO FROM HERE?

OVER 100 women attended an anarchist feminist conference in London on the weekend of 7-8 December. The conference was organised by women from Spain, Austria and the USA as well as Britain, with men taking charge of the crèche and helping with refreshments. The list of pre-arranged workshops ranged from astrology, meditation and life drawing to use of video, body-making, self-defence and attitudes to violence, and women in prison.

Among both organisers and participants there was disagreement on the usefulness of a separate meeting at Conway Hall between women and men as 'leaders in the anarchist movement', and if anyone had hoped to keep discussion confined to that subject they were to be disappointed. By the end of the evening what seemed, to me at any rate, to be a central question, remained unanswered: were many anarchist women themselves helping to reinforce sexism, by being little or no part in anarchist, as opposed to feminist, groups and activities?

In other words, did the anarchist movement actually matter to them?

One woman agreed that she was not involved in the local anarchist group because she automatically assumed that the men should be left to get on with it. A second said she had never been to an anarchist meeting because she felt more confident with other women. A third complained about the lack of feminist content in papers like FREEDOM, but was unable to suggest what there should do when it was pointed out that many women preferred anyway to work for women's or exclusively anarcha-feminist papers and newsletters.

How should we invent out of this vicious circle? Is a future possible in which the anarchist movement in this country is split in two along sexist lines, with women clawing to be the only true anarchists and men accusing them of introspection?

Perhaps others will think this a more suitable question for the feminist sociology class. At any rate, the actual discussion did not deal with it but drifted chaotically around matters in general. Much of it got bogged down in a hopeless sort of exchange between one group of men and another, caused by one or two men resenting the fact that members of a Men Against Sexism group spoke in soft tones with middle class accents, and had been to university. One joked by shouting several times over that everything had been FUCKING BORING.

All this was and became a desire to learn something from the meeting was shown by the large turnout. In my view it could have got somewhere had the organisers tried to get some form and structure to it. To many anarchists this seems an instant an idea that they must break instead into half a dozen or so small groups, mostly consisting (as was pointed out at the time) of their own friends or other like-minded comrades — a move which completely defeats the possibility of a substantive debate.

The same 'tyranny of structurelessness' criticism can also be made at the main part of the conference, which was held in the great, gloomy halls of the Centro Iberico in Harrow Road. There were too many different topics to choose from, time for many groups meeting at once to get nowhere (so had to function little trusats from the crèche). Noise ruined concentration, and again people began to split into subgroups, which made things yet more difficult.

Another disadvantage was that there was scarcely any time for plenary sessions, where women who had come to an anarchist meeting for the first time could find out more about anarchism itself before the workshops started. The last workshop of the conference, 'Anarcha-feminism: Where do we go from here?' could have been split into two parts, with the first session as the first meeting. For instance, there could have been a general discussion on the differences between revolutionary, radical, socialist and anarchist feminisms; this could have helped to clarify ideas before the participants embarked on specific topics.

Very possibly the number of workshops stemmed from the fact that this was the first conference for such a long time. Inevitably then the most valuable part of the meeting consisted of establishment of contact between people gathered together from all parts of the country. There were also women from Spain, including the Catalan part, Maria Pea-terudom, and a member of Women Against Imperialism, who talked about the women's movements in Northern Ireland and the Irish Republic, and in particular about women in Armagh prison.

This was an informative and, naturally enough, provocative session. Women Against Imperialism are calling on all feminists, including anarchists, to "build a campaign around political prisoners in Armagh Gaol", fighting for political status. This raises the immediate difficulty for anarchists of supporting a campaign which would lead to a greater liberty among prisoners rather than demanding better conditions for all prisoners, as well as questioning the grounds of their imprisonment in the first place.

Another point is that of women supporting the IRA at all, and parallels were made with the Leninists of Soviet Russia and Islamic revolutionaries of Iran.

I have referred mainly, and deliberately, to what I saw as weaknesses of the conference. Being, however, one and noticeable, I was not able to attend all workshops, some of which were undoubtedly of interest and practical help. Nor have I mentioned the music, dancing and feminist films. There was a general feeling that the conference should be followed shortly by another, probably outside London, and probably to develop more fully some of the themes that arose. This was an encouraging sign of the women's success as a catalyst, and the organisers are to be thanked for the work and effort they put into it.

GAA

SOLVING HELPLESSNESS

My memory of meetings is appellingly bad - and even if it were not, I'm sure that my account of the evening session of the Anarcha-Feminist conference would be so biased as to be positively misleading for those who didn't attend and trembling for those whose views I chose to recount.

However, I would like to comment on a contribution made at the meeting which I believe was important. One woman (I think one of the facilitators/organisers) pointed out that she had, by implication, other women found it difficult to involve herself in the production of a/an anarchist magazine. The impression I received (not necessarily the one given out) was that of helplessness to that,whilst the problem was clearly outlined, no attempts (or request) was made to solve it.

Helplessness is something I would wish on my enemies, but not on anyone who supports (or at least, does not actively oppose) anarchist ideas. It is a truly pessimistic condition in that it implies an individual who is powerless to act, being enslaved or determined by forces 'beyond his or her control'.

But need helplessness be permanent? The answer, if we are to be optimistic

Anarchist-Feminist Conference (*Freedom* 40, no. 23, 22 December 1979)

they wanted. Funnily enough for anarchists, they wanted us to follow their rules—a bit of a paradox! They were so busy wrangling among themselves while I was bothered by punks getting beaten up at gigs. They just had no interest at all."

The earliest confirmed gig at Harrow Road in the Centro Iberico era, was Saturday 21 October 1978 featuring Raped, Northern Ireland's Rudi, and the 'A.U.M. Band,' who may have been the Anarcho Utopian Mystics political group.[2] The squatters were not necessarily any more aligned with the punks than they were with the traditional anarchists. Faebhean Kwest, guitarist with Raped, states: "the people in charge had nothing really in common with us, except it was a place to play."

Brian Young (Rudi): We moved to London in August '78 with all our gear, the four band members, my wife Liz, and Gavin Martin—an *Alternative Ulster* zine writer trying out for *NME*—all sleeping in the van until we found a squat in Clapham. We met Raped and became pals, they got us lots of gigs, and Alan Hauser was their manager, he arranged the Centro Iberico gigs for us. The first gig was a benefit for Persons Unknown and we had to cart our gear up several flights of stairs into what looked like an old classroom. There was no PA so Dennis Forbes from Pretty Boy Floyd drove back to Clapham and hired us theirs for £25, while the Spanish certainly made us welcome with lots of free wine. There was a review by Dave McCullough in the *Alternative Ulster* zine which he told us he wrote as "an incentive"! It said, "saw Rudi at the Iberico Club and found them atrocious!" Our second gig was for Guy Fawkes Night, 5 November. Some of our mates travelled down from Watford so we had a great time and, this time, didn't take advantage of the refreshments until after we'd played.

It made sense as a music venue given the former assembly hall on the first floor and the old gymnasium on the ground could each hold several hundred attendees. A consistent event schedule commenced with all but one known date 1978–1981

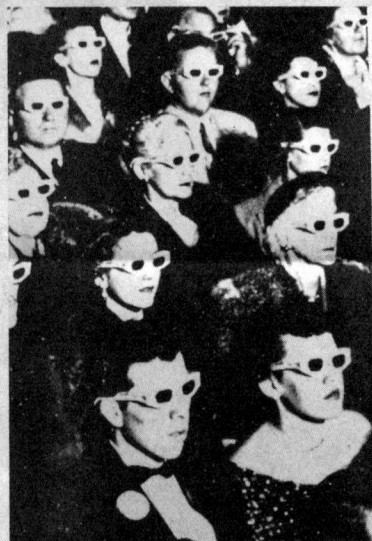

SATURDAY 21st OCTOBER '78

RAPED!!

Rudi + A.U.M. Band

admission £1.   Open 8pm   at Centro Iberico, Old School,
421a Harrow Road, W9.

Rudi, Raped, and the A.U.M. Band,
Saturday 21 October 1978

SUNDAY, NOVEMBER 5, 1978

RUDI + FOUR KINGS

(new wave groups)

at 4 p.m.
Centro Iberico (Old School)
421 A HARROW RD. LONDON W.9.

Underground:Westbourne Park
Buses: 28,31

ADMISION £1.

photo acknoleage to The Society of the Spectacle ,
guy debord, Detroit, 1977.

Viva ETA, GRAPO, CNT-FAI,Copel,La independencia de Euskadi y de
las Islas Canarias,El Gobierno de la Republica Espanola,El Gobierno Basko y la Generalitat de Catalunya en el Exilio,Las Honorables
Patrullas de Control, la Masoneria Catalana y la Gran Logia de Ori-
ente,la Liberacion de la Mariguana, de la Pedofilia,de los Gay y de
las Lesbianas y vivan todas las minorias de la Peninsula.....

Gobierno RepublicaEspanola y Generalitat de Catalunya:155HARLEY RD.
                                              LONDON NW 1o.

Rudi and the Four Kings, Sunday 5 November 1978 (Courtesy of Brian Young)

taking place on a weekend. This was out of consideration for people's working lives, school or college studies, the need to keep the peace and not provoke noise complaints from neighbouring streets.

The venue was a full-time home for up to a dozen individuals at its peak with rooms on the second and third floors becoming living space despite the lack of running water, heating, and unusably derelict areas. Ignorant recalls: "You'd go off the main corridor and you'd be in these empty rooms with no electricity falling over things." While many rooms had been cleared, others retained the traditional school desk set up and others had been used to store old furnishings. Eduardo Niebla, a Spanish musician who played the Glastonbury Festival in 1979 as part of Mother Gong, was invited to play at the centre that year after which he was invited to move in.

> **Eduardo Niebla:** I was doing gigs around London and, being Spanish, the guys at Centro Iberico contacted me and told me they were doing a lot of events and, if I wanted, I could become a part of it. They organised a concert for me and soon I was living there. I divided a classroom at the top of the building into four areas so I had a bed, a space where my girlfriend used to write, another area for eating and things like that, then a practice space for my music. I had a string going out of the window all the way to the bottom outside with a metal tin attached at my end so people would pull it, it'd make a noise, and I could go let them in. The older Spanish guys didn't live there, they had their own places and were really kind. This old Galician gentleman would allow us to come to his place and have a shower or a bath.
>
> Asensio and Salvatore were arranging the schedule of activities: they were regularly putting on films and hosting discussions about them. I knew a lot of artists so would invite people I played with. Sometimes, at two or three in the morning, my friend would pull the string to get me out

Rudi and the Four Kings, Sunday 5 November 1978 (Courtesy of Brian Young)

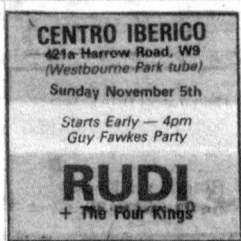

CENTRO IBERICO
421a Harrow Road, W9
(Westbourne Park tube)

Sunday November 5th

Starts Early — 4pm
Guy Fawkes Party

RUDI
+ The Four Kings

The sheds and cottage across the playground with the woodyard behind (Courtesy of William Orbit)

Entrance from the school playground (Courtesy of Laurie Mayer)

The exit to Harrow Road (Courtesy of William Orbit)

Carefree quiet days for one man and his dog (Courtesy of William Orbit)

of bed and I'd lean out of the window. "Eduardo! I have a session for you! Come on! Get your guitar!" There were all sorts of musicians would play: folk, jazz, rock, members of the London Philharmonic and New York Philharmonic—a lot of high quality and more basic music.

We helped people making films as well as visual artists: they would come and use the building as a studio and we got some local guys to turn a space into a studio for photography. We were not directly involved in politics but we would help anyone who needed it. In Spain, you could not have an abortion, so girls would come and we would support them. Bands would store equipment with us: one Italian guy said, "I need somewhere to put a piano!" so we told him he could bring it to us—he's now famous and all the best venues bring him their pianos or rent his when people tour Italy. People would need somewhere to stay so we hosted scientists, people from universities who would give talks for us, anarchists from Spain would come; people would gather, very intelligent people, and they would all always have stories to tell.

Lea Nicholson: I visited with John Lane and we met Eduardo. It was intriguing, someone living there, this big building, having that much space in London was ridiculous! I remember thinking, "This would be quite a pleasant place to live." Strangely, there were still desks in certain classrooms and we sat on them as we talked. It reminded me of properties that are abandoned and left just as they are until some urban explorer goes in twenty to thirty years later—quite weird!

Another curious feature was the former caretaker's cottage at the opposite side of the schoolyard. The musician William Orbit attended a party in the cottage in 1976 while visiting from Amsterdam. Then, returning to the UK permanently in 1977, he learned the cottage was available and received a key from a friend.

Grant Gilbert in the decayed part of the school (Courtesy of Laurie Mayer)

William Orbit: There was no one there except for one guy living in one of the little rooms so I pretty much had it to myself. It was in a terrible state, but I cleaned it up and called my girlfriend: "Come on over, we can live here!" The cottage backed onto a woodyard and had a little ring-fenced area so children in the playground couldn't get right up to the front door, and there was a small private garden between the cottage and the street. There were two doors, one into the ringfencing and one direct onto the playground which we'd use.

Requiring better accommodation once his girlfriend gave birth, Orbit moved out, whereupon Grant Gilbert, an old school friend, and his new wife, Laurie Mayer, moved in having immigrated from the US. A year later, with the breakup of his relationship, Orbit returned to Harrow Road and the resident trio formed Torch Song and set up the first iteration of Guerilla Studios.

Laurie Mayer: The house had a cottage vibe but the layout was such that it felt spacious. Bedroom, living room, kitchen, bathroom downstairs, two bedrooms upstairs—one of which became the studio. There was no hot water when we moved in; the previous residents would heat water in pans on the stove. We had a friend who was a gas fitter and he hooked up a water heater for us. We didn't have a phone for the first year and relied on a phone box just outside.

William Orbit: When I first visited they were just setting up shop in the school, but when I moved in a year later they were well and truly going. Two-thirds of the edifice was empty and never got occupied because the roof had fallen in and it was in quite a state; no one would go in there because it was a bit of a dangerous place. It was such a contrast with the Centro part which they kept immaculate! With derelict buildings, the windows get smashed: people only smash windows when they don't think anybody is

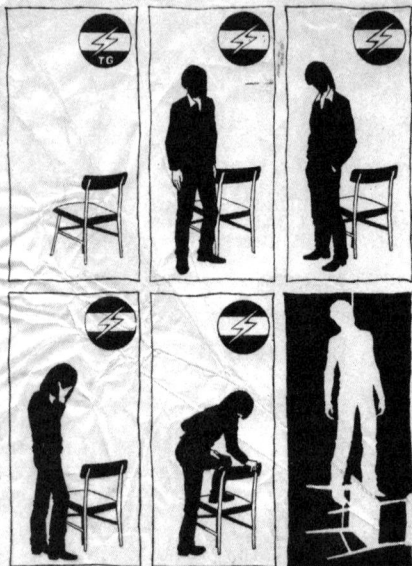

Throbbing Gristle, Sunday 21 January
1979 (Courtesy of Jordi Valls)

there. The Centro Iberico had all its windows because the lights were on and it was clearly occupied. There were all these interestingly shaped rooms. They were sort of square with very high ceilings, all sorts of odd-shaped rooms in this warren-like building. The furnishings were gone because the wood was so good, when wood got scarce you couldn't buy wood without knots. I liked to make things out of wood and the best wood was always from an old school desk or something like that because the wood didn't have knots in it. People would have had that. Bricks, wood, lead pipe—I think people had taken all of that kind of thing because you would get decent money for it.

Next door to the squat was the secondhand shop run by Giuseppe and Raymundo, Gus and Ray's, it was next to the woodyard the cottage backed onto. Half the shop was just musical instruments, so I basically bought the lot and filled the squat with tons of different instruments. You'd find these dusty old things in the shop and I'd just say, "I'll have them, mate!" and give them some cash: trumpets, protosynths, keyboards ...

A further feature of the site was the series of basic storage sheds at the rear of the playground backing onto the canal. Unaware that the school had doubled as a centre for adult vocational training, the new residents were rather mystified why primary and junior school children might have required such well-furnished workshops and such a quantity of equipment.

William Orbit: It really was a bit of a ghost town; it was like they just walked out. When we were very short of money one time, we borrowed Grant's mother's car and got loads of metal from the workshops, hefted it into his car and drove it to a scrapyard. We actually damaged the axle doing it because we had so much metal, so many tools and other things—it made such a terrible noise! They didn't have any of the big lathes (those are very valuable) and they'd taken

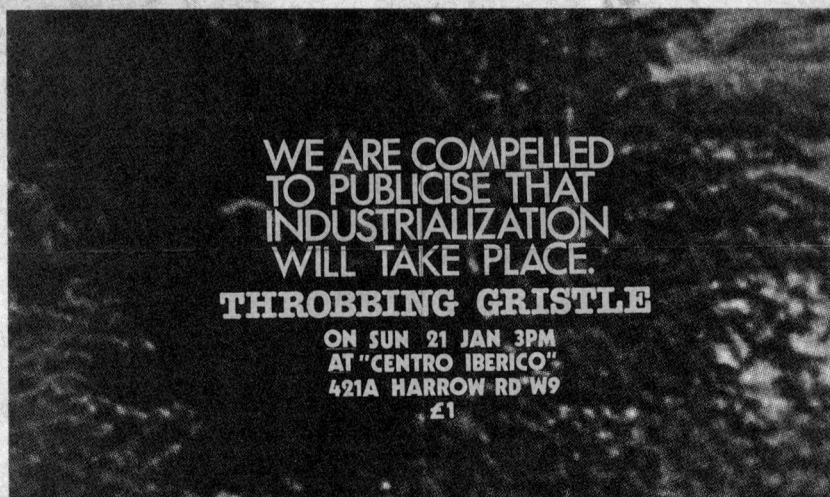

Throbbing Gristle, Sunday 21 January
1979 (Courtesy of Jordi Valls)

the power tools, but lots of small tools and bits of metal had been discarded in these sheds.

The shop next door, the alarm might go on all night, so one night Laurie and I went down and got all the paint from the old paint stores in the school and we splashed it all over their windows because we were so annoyed at it keeping us awake. Of course, the next day we saw some poor staff member cleaning up and we felt very ashamed of ourselves.

The group maintained cordial relations with their neighbours, arranging a gig in Centro Iberico for Rico Conning's group, The Lines, sometime in 1979 with the venue still fairly bare: "My memory is of a big, cavernous, well … abandoned … school assembly hall. The sound and backline were predictably horrendous—par for the course for a gig of that type. We didn't pack it out but on word of mouth it was still reasonably attended." An article in 1979 referred to "the great, gloomy halls of the Centro Iberico." Laurie Mayer confirms: "It was stunning to look at: crumbling and gothic with flaming oil cans for heat. There was a whole section with the roof missing, floor covered in rubble with weeds growing out of it." While the residents would make small improvements, the overall integrity of the building would continue to deteriorate over time.

William Orbit: We weren't joined at the hip with our friends across the way, but it was a golden time. We did get very friendly with Eduardo and his girlfriend, an opera singer. Eduardo's bedroom was very nice, a funny-shaped room he'd repurposed from being a classroom—they'd even made their own bunk beds. One time I came back and Eduardo was looking grim and crying. What had happened was one of our musical friends in North London, he had a rabbit called William and his girlfriend wrote a note saying, "William has died!" and it went to Eduardo. He and his girlfriend had gone over to the cottage telling everyone I'd died then I get back wondering why everyone was so upset and why they were all so happy to see me!

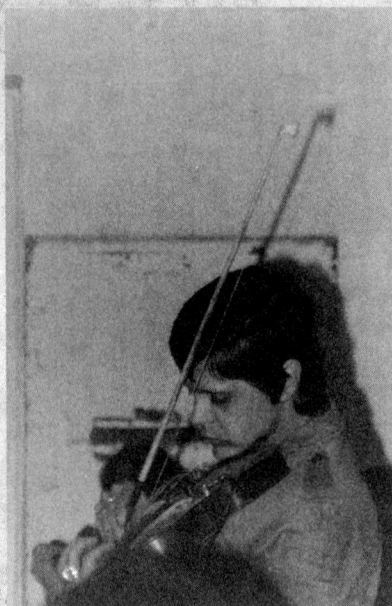

Genesis P-Orridge at Centro Iberico, 21 January 1979 (Courtesy of Kevin Thorne)

There was also a guy called Mr. Dreadlocks who was a sort of vagrant. He was clearly psychotic, he would talk to himself. But he was always smiling—more a happy psychotic. He would live in the metal workshop at the back. Other than Eduardo and his girlfriend and Mr. Dreadlocks, I don't think there were many permanent residents because, as accommodation, the school was just too basic. People would maybe doss down there; there'd be comings and goings and we'd see everything from the window; we'd hear the gate clang; but it was quite quiet at the time. I had a dog I'd let run around in the playground, then these events would happen and tons of people would pour in and pour out.

There were two 1981 shows for Torch Song, the first around June, the second on 14 July as Mayer describes: "We were friends with Swamp Children (later, Kalima) and got them to come from Manchester and stay. Wind Up Ensemble was actually us, a ridiculous name we had used before. That gig was such a success, so many people came, that we had about twenty people sleeping all over the house." Rico Conning puts Centro Iberico's growing reputation down to the fact, "Throbbing Gristle had bestowed their unmistakable cool on the venue.... The vibe was kind of a postpunk version of some of the London raves that occurred ten years later."[3] Catalan artist Jordi Valls, an associate of TG, was the key connect.

Jordi Valls: I heard of Centro Iberico through my friend Eliseu Huertas Cos. Eliseu told me they had this area for live music, projecting films, with a nice bar for sandwiches, coffee, tea, and beer. I showed Genesis P-Orridge the place for a TG live-action and he loved it.... We had an incredible network of UK and international addresses we picked up from music magazines and fanzines so I sent out hundreds of flyers I had designed on my kitchen table. I also designed the £1 tickets for the door.

Poison Girls, Disco Students, Eratics,
Friday 14 March 1980

The Eduardo Niebla Band,
Sunday 30 March 1980
(Courtesy of Eduardo Niebla)

On Sunday 21 January 1979, during a harsh cold spell, around 180 people braved wintry conditions for a 3:00 p.m. show. Bonfires were built inside the venue both for warmth and to enhance the intense atmosphere with Philip Sanderson (founder of the Snatch Tapes label and the Storm Bugs group) explaining, "that gig was bitterly cold, but great—not sure the fires warmed the place up so much as becoming a 'real' smoke machine!" Those who arrived early witnessed COUM Transmissions' twenty-minute film, *After Cease to Exist*, notorious for a core sequence in which Chris Carter is tied down to a table for special treatment by Cosey Fanni Tutti and her collaborator, punk icon Soo Catwoman.

> **Jim Thirlwell**: That was an incredible fucking show. It was in the winter, really cold, and there was a long line out in the playground. They started playing while people were still filing in, so we were already missing it, then I got in and it was still freezing cold. From memory, once we were all in, they locked the door so no one could get out. There was this foul-smelling gas put out into the audience, then this harsh and confrontational music, really aggressive and propulsive in a way I hadn't seen before. Then they showed this famous castration film—everyone who had seen it the first time looked away because it was so gross.

> **Eliseu Huertas Cos**: I was running the film club at the Antonio Machado so when TG told me they had a film to show, I said no problem. I opened a hole in the wall so I could project my 16mm projector over their heads onto the backdrop. The film was spliced with cheap Sellotape and as soon as I started the projector the image was uncontrollable. Someone was telling me we needed to start so I stuck my finger between the lens and the film which was enough to get it going. It was bloody amazing! Someone was being castrated!

The band went on to perform precisely one hour, the rule at all their live shows, which included the band ad-libbing what

Eduardo Niebla on stage at Centro Iberico, May 1980 (Courtesy of Eduardo Niebla)

would become their song 'Persuasion.' P-Orridge then offered to show the film again for latecomers.

> **Cosey Fanni Tutti (Throbbing Gristle):** As Throbbing Gristle was very much supportive of antiestablishment communities and those who struggled, the anarchists there were very much of interest though we didn't have much contact. We purposely looked for interesting, odd places not on the gig circuit and tried to avoid universities too. Of course, we also had the added motivation that regular venues wouldn't have us! Centro Iberico was a large, open space, we don't recall a stage, just people milling around, a big space with a lot of people but not ram-packed, a casual atmosphere and very much like a squat—not disorganised, but not a regular venue or stage set up. Someone did light an open fire which was a crazy idea, though pretty necessary because it was freezing cold due to there being no heating!

Between 1979 and 1981, a significant array of groups associated with the London underground scene performed while the individuals involved continued to maintain links to various parts of the political underground of the new punk anarchist era. Steve Lake recounts:

> **Steve Lake:** I was going out with this Spanish girl, Conchita, and she had quite a few friends around there who were all, kind of, anarchists. There was Elizabeth—sadly now dead; she was friends with David Morris from the McLibel case—a big feminist contingent and a few separatist women's houses arranging health care and abortions for Spanish women. I knew the school on Harrow Road because we used to do free gigs at Meanwhile Gardens in Westbourne Park or at Acklam Hall. Someone told me the Basques had their own separate bit upstairs. There were probably good reasons but, at the time, I thought, "Oh, we're anarchists but we're still separating?" Doing gigs there, we would only

Inner City Unit, Androids of Mu, Door and the Window,
Saturday 10 May 1980 (Courtesy of Drusilla Verney and Tom
Vague)

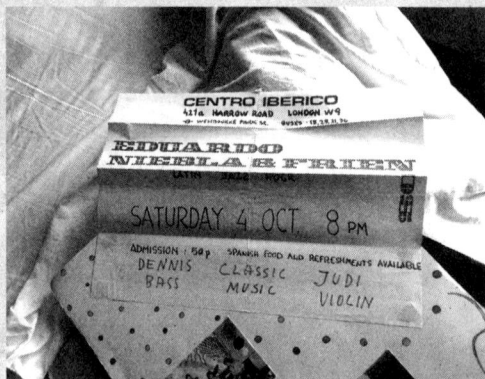

Eduardo Niebla and Friends,
Saturday 4 October 1980
(Courtesy of Eduardo Niebla)

Eric Random, Swamp Children,
and The Wind-Up Ensemble,
Tuesday 14 July 1981

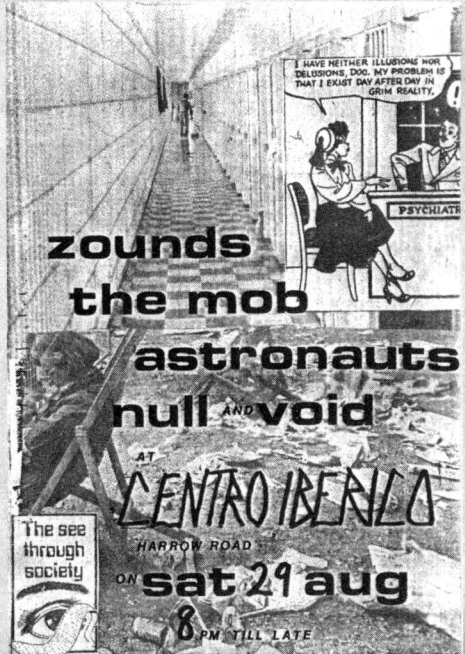

Zounds, The Mob,
The Astronauts, and Null and
Void, Saturday 29 August 1981

Second annual Peña Portobello
Fiesta de la Poesía y la Música
(Courtesy of Eduardo Niebla)

Third annual Peña Portobello
Fiesta de la Poesía y la Música
(Courtesy of Eduardo Niebla)

ever see one or two of them, a couple of older guys who seemed almost like caretakers. Places like this were always pretty spartan but it was very free: you'd come in, set up, do what you wanted. Nobody bothered you and there was never any trouble.[4]

Eduardo Niebla: There was a gentleman with a place on Portobello and we would bring things to him for printing, then spread leaflets around, little posters in the shops, and so on. We got very nice audiences. We had a small bar and you could serve whatever you wanted. There was an honesty box, and people used to make coffee or tea for everyone, but it had to stop because a new generation of guys came in and there wasn't enough money in the box sometimes. People would get a drink without putting money there, but it was a nice thought.

Alongside this new role as a gig venue, it retained links to its past through support for several anarchist events. The London Workers' Group organised an all-night party on 6 October 1979 to celebrate the hundredth anniversary of the birth of anarchist martyr Joe Hill, which was described in a later write-up as a mellow soiree for which "two bands supplied the music and scrumptious food was provided." A three-day anarcho-feminist conference then took place across 7–9 December with around one hundred attendees taking in films, dancing, and workshops on everything from astrology to meditation to self-defence.[5]

The presence of a strong Spanish contingent, determined to live up to the name of their adopted home, also led to a variety of events sharing Spanish art and culture. There was a showing of Buñuel's *Ensayo de un crimen*, a film by Walerian Borowczyk, and a concert by 'Monsieur and Madame Kabal' on 29 March 1980; numerous performances by Niebla and friends; and in July 1980 and June 1981 respectively, the venue staged the second and third annual Peña Portobello Fiesta de la Poesía y la Música.[6]

Letters

Dear Comrades,

My name is Ronan Bennett. When I was 18 I was lifted and charged with armed robbery and shooting a policeman. The judge gave me 10 years for the robbery and life for the murder. I am a member of the Irish Republican Socialist Party.

My main purpose in writing is to ask you to help me establish contact with anyone sharing your politics who would be willing to swop a few letters with me here in the most naked manifestation of Britain's fascism. Just one requirement — it has to be a woman. I'm afraid that Irish women are still too much under the thumb of the Church, the State, their parents, their husbands and each other. To them we are just daft lads who ought to have picked up spades instead of M18s. Perhaps I'd better explain further why I want a female anarchist to write. Well it's partly because, as I said before, women here just don't seem interested in the struggle. It's also partly perhaps obviously, because long periods of exclusively male society can have a bad effect — you tend to become aggressive and too insensitive. Any contact at all with a woman is relieving to say the least, and helps you remember you're still human.

Another thing. In jail we have organised ourselves into communes which act as productive and social units. We have a Prisoners Revolutionary Commune which turns out the best of gear in the way of leather goods which are expertly modelled. Our problem is finding markets. The money we get goes to a welfare fund to buy anoraks, jeans and boots for us this winter. If you know of anyone who wants wallets, purses, bags,etc, let me know and we'll supply.

Thanks, Ronan Bennett, Cage 14, Long Kesh, Co. Antrim, N. Ireland.

Ronan Bennett writes (August 1975)

PERSONS UNKNOWN

In the meantime, events crucial to the future of the resurrected Centro Iberico were playing out in the form of the 'Persons Unknown' trial. Police concerns regarding the danger represented by Britain's anarchists had never abated after what the authorities felt was an unsatisfactory conclusion to the Angry Brigade trial. The anarchists, meanwhile, saw official forces and the press using them as bogeymen to create false anxiety and justify repression.

Back in 1974, Ronan Bennett, a member of the Irish Republican Socialist Party, was convicted of murdering a Royal Ulster Constabulary officer during a robbery on behalf of the Official Irish Republican Army. During his imprisonment, a letter from him was published in *Black Flag*. It requested a female anarchist pen pal and led to a response from Iris Mills, a New Zealand–born supporter of the Anarchist Black Cross living in Huddersfield.[1] Bennett was released in 1975 after his conviction was ruled unsafe and, following threats from loyalist paramilitaries, he moved in with Mills and her husband around April 1976.

Imaginations ran wild within the security services who now feared an IRA-anarchist alliance. Having been placed under surveillance, Mills and Bennett were arrested on 11 May 1977 under the Prevention of Terrorism Act, then released. With the police attempting to have Bennett deported, the pair fled briefly to Paris, then to London where they were rearrested on 24 May. This was the start of a rolling wave of around eighty raids by the Anti-Terrorist Squad on anarchist-affiliated addresses. Dafydd 'Taff' Ladd was arrested on 2 June; Stewart Carr on 12 June; Vincent Stevenson, who had helped set up a support group

Huddersfield Raid: Ronan Bennet Released

On 11 May Special Branch officers arrested Iris Mills and Ronan Bennet at the old Black Flag address in Huddersfield on a warrant issued under the Prevention of Terrorism Act. Iris was released following an intensive campaign on her behalf after seven days, but Ronan was served with an Exclusion Order and it was only due to prompt local and national solidarity that this order was revoked and Ronan released from custody. Iris takes up the story:

On Wednesday 11th May at 7 a.m. our house in Huddersfield was raided by Special Branch. They forced their way in without warrants and declared that we were being held under the "Prevention of Terrorism Act" and that the house would be searched for explosives, whereupon a fat brown dog dutifully sniffed at the skirting boards but found nothing!

We were taken to the local police station and there we had our photos taken as well as our fingerprints. At first Ronan refused to give his fingerprints but was told they would break his arm if necessary. Moreover, repeated requests to see a lawyer were refused.

From the start of the interrogation it was clear that we were being held because of our anarchist beliefs, and that Ronan was specially picked on because he was Irish. We were never accused of any "terrorist" acts either past/ present or future and there was never any suggestion of charges being made against us under the Act. We were continually asked about our political thoughts. Questions were also asked regarding various groups namely the S.L.A., I.W.W. and the A.W.A.

At times the questioning took on farcical aspects, for instance I was asked if I was an anarchist. Having answered 'yes' I was told 'so you're a self confessed anarchist'! Ronan was told that he was known to have mixed with bombers, robbers and others of ill-repute whilst in prison!

At first we were held for two days, we were questioned on the Wednesay but left completely alone on Thursday. Then on Friday we were told that because of our unco-operative behaviour we would be held for a further five days.

A friend of ours who called at the house meanwhile, intending to stay for a few days, was also picked up and held for two days. He had phoned before coming and had been informed by someone (the police) who answered the phone that we were out but would be back later. However, his detention turned out to be a lucky break for us. After our friend was released on the Sunday he immediately contacted the N.C.C.L. who in turn contacted a well-known local solicitor, Mr. Barrington Black, who secured my release almost immediately.

Unfortunately Ronan was recommended for deportation back to Northern Ireland as he was Irish and had incurred the wrath of the 'chief' Special Branch Investigator, by refusing to answer questions and by refusing to be intimidated. It seems his 'crimes' amounted to being Irish, anarchist and rude to the police.

The only 'evidence' against us apparently was our literature, one questioner went on about the 'bloody anarchist/revolutionary books' in almost hysterical agitation. Also I discovered to my horror, when I got home that they had set up a shooting gallery in our attic and had so placed various items, such as an air-pistol, crossbow, old ex-army shoulder bags, a pack and pots and pans to suggest a para-military camp.

All this time (seven days) we were held in the cells at the local Huddersfield station. We had no contact with outside world or with each other (except for two brief meetings on the Wednesday and the following Tuesday). The food was appalling (inedible at times) and totally inadequate. We were kept in the cells without any exercise for twenty four hours a day and the lights were left on continuously day and night.

On Tuesday evening Ronan was moved to Armley prison in Leeds. There he was held in solitary confinement, as a Category 'A' prisoner, which meant that he was locked up for twenty three (sometimes twenty four) hours each day. On the following Monday he was transferred to Brixton prison in London in order to meet a representative of the Home Office, to put his request for the Exclusion Order to be revoked. This representative was a Q.C., Mr. Ronald Waterhouse, who asked Ronan a series of questions. These questions differed little from those that Special Branch had already asked i.e. Ronan's background in Northern Ireland -- he stated that he had been a supporter (though not a member) of the Official Sinn Fein and when in Long Kesh had supported the I.R.S.P. He was then asked questions about his and my present political views. These he refused to answer saying that this was not relevant to the 'Prevention of Terrorism Act' and on this point he was backed up by his lawyer, maintaining that people should not be punished for their ideas alone.

It seems on afterthought that I was only held to prevent news on Ronan's detention from being leaked, which also explains why our friend who came to visit was held. Because the questioning was surprisingly brief (about four hours at most for each of us) it also seems that they had made up their minds as to Ronan's deportation from the beginning.

On a more sinister aspect, one of the interrogators at Huddersfield police station, a Steve Thompson, denied that he was a policeman or a member of Special Branch. When asked if he was a member of some intelligence service he refused to answer.

The so-called 'temporary' Prevention of Terrorism Act is another 'lawful' infringement by the State on the liberties of its citizens. It is a means by which the police, for reasons which they don't have to specify, can pick up anyone at all and hold them incommunicado for at least seven days -- longer if they wish. This was the most disturbing aspect of our case -- that we were held for so long without any of our friends realising what had happened.

Its claim to 'prevent' terrorism is dubious to say the least, for instance it didn't prevent the Balcombe Street Siege. About 2,500 people have been picked up under the Act and of these only 11 have been found guilty of any offences. The most important point, from the police angle, is that it enables them to hold anyone and go through their personal effects and to build up a file of intelligence information nationwide.

Iris Mills and friend

Bennett and Mills arrested (*Black Flag* IV, no. 15, May 1977)

for those arrested, was himself arrested outside the Rising Free bookshop—the support group's address—on 4 July; then Trevor Dawton, a student staying at Stevenson's flat, on 7 July. The charges were serious, yet vague: "conspiring with persons known and unknown" to cause explosions.[2]

Things started to go wrong for the police from the very start. As an example of how flawed their intelligence was, on 26 July a raid targeted Centro Iberico ... at its old address, 83a Haverstock Hill! The surprised bouncers guarding the basement gambling club proceeded to have a pitched battle with the plainclothes officers in the belief this was an attack by some rival gang. Meanwhile, police identity parades failed; support group members were harassed; the police were even permitted to search a defence lawyer and read their confidential papers.

Everyone involved was aware that Carr had no affiliation with anarchism and had been picked up only because he knew Mills and Ladd. He disassociated himself from the 'political' trial entirely, voiced his disagreement with the others' politics, admitted to vague plans to commit armed robbery, and was tried separately. That did not stop the police from using the association to dig themselves out of a hole when on 16 November, the attorney general, Samuel Silkin, refused permission to proceed with the bombing charges. The police had declined to present charges to the Crown Prosecution Service, insisting on speaking to the attorney general in the hope they'd have a better chance of getting their desired outcome. The prosecution now used Carr's self-incrimination to substitute 'conspiracy to rob' as the charge against all six.

At Lambeth Magistrates Court, the police were reprimanded for deliberately delaying the remand hearings which ultimately took seven months rather than the normal few weeks. Embarrassingly, the prosecution's evidence was so slender that every one of these 'dangerous' defendants received bail: Dawton on 28 September; Mills on 26 October; Stevenson on 11 December; Ladd on 21 December though police pressure on his sureties meant it was 1 March before he was released; and Bennett on 16

More Harassment

Two comrades Iris Mills and Ronan Bennett were picked up on May 11th under the Prevention of Terrorism Act (P.T.A.), after the Special Branch raided their home in Huddersfield at 7 o'clock in the morning. Under the P.T.A. people can be held for up to seven days without being charged. Iris and Ronan are both involved with the Anarchist Black Cross, and have also been active in the Murrays Defence Campaign. After being held for six days Iris was released on Tuesday 17th — no charges were brought against her. After Ronan's detention however, the police asked Home Secretary Rees to serve an exclusion on him, which Rees dutifully did.

Ronan came over to England last April from Ireland, and if his appeal against the exclusion order is turned down he will be forced to return to the Irish Republic. This attack by the police is the latest of a long line in which the P.T.A. has been used, especially against the Irish community. Since the P.T.A. was introduced over 2,200 people have been detained, over 100 deported and 1100 have been detained at ports of entry whilst coming from Ireland. Of all those detained less than 30 have been convicted for political offences. The Act so far has been used to terrorise the Irish community — it can be used against other groups just as easily.

At the time of going to press we don't know if Ronan has been deported, but for further information contact Black Cross, 123 Upper Tollington Park, London N4 ☐ Peter Webb.

Bennett and Mills arrested (*Zero* no. 1, June 1977)

August 1979.[3] Further shenanigans saw fraud charges introduced then dropped; accusations that the police planted evidence; the jury vetted by the prosecution with no such right for the defence; then the entire jury replaced after a critical article in *The Guardian* was deemed to prejudice proceedings.

This became the cause célèbre bringing together anarchists and punks. The 'Persons Unknown' support group turned to the punks to mobilise numbers, voices, and cash. The police would even refer to the group as 'PUNK' in their reports—a conjoining of 'P-Unk' which no one involved with the cause noticed or used. The first meeting of Persons Unknown took place at the Rising Free bookshop on 13 June and the first benefit on 15 July at Conway Hall, with another at the same venue on 29 September. Fundraising was initially slow: the treasurer's flat was burgled in November with October's donations stolen; a sum of £30 plus cheques.[4]

Deepening involvement from the punk scene had an impact. A gig at North London Polytechnic on 11 January 1979 saw The Soft Boys, The Passions, and Charge Resisters bring in £220 after expenses from three hundred attendees. Crass then got involved bringing their substantial following along. As Penny Rimbaud recounts: "It was Ronan Bennett who contacted us. He explained his situation and then visited so we could discuss possibilities. First of all, we wanted to be sure that we believed he was innocent! We then suggested doing a gig with profits going to the defence fund. My close friend Wally (Hope)—I organised the first Stonehenge Festival with him—was murdered by the state so I was very aware of the kind of skulduggery that was going on." Steve Ignorant recalls that they had already heard about the trial: "The Persons Unknown thing came to our attention through Freedom Press in Whitechapel who were distributing some stuff for us at the time. The whole thing looked very dodgy so we thought a benefit gig would be a good idea to support the cause." Crass were even interviewed for *Black Flag* in July 1979, quite a feat given the ongoing hostility of the traditional anarchists to punk 'interlopers.'

Iris Mills and Ronan Bennett were re-arrested in London on May 24th. They had previously been detained under the Prevention of Terrorism Act in Huddersfield, went before a tribunal, were thoroughly examined as to their views and activities, and totally cleared. They were again detained under the PTA, but as the procedure was the same, when a friend telephoned them and was answered by an assumed human voice saying they had "gone away for the weekend" he guessed what had happened (last time the voice invited him up — and he came and was detained). He telephoned around and we were able to notify a solicitor. The detention was cancelled and they were charged instead.

Next day headlines in the press announced:
BOMB MATERIAL SEIZED IN HUNT FOR ANARCHISTS.

The "hunted anarchists" had only a week before gathered in public demonstrations and meetings (over the May 1st weekend) and our group had later held a social, only a week before the "hunt". Anarchists were (one paper said) about to "attack London!" What could be "an important anarchist cell" on the "lines of the Angry Brigade" was announced by the Telegraph, and the shock-horror stories were on. "A hunt was on today for members of an anarchist group thought to be planning a new bomb wave in London" (News) "on lines of the Angry Brigade", a theme

stated over and over again and obviously coming from the police (oddly enough coinciding with the end of certain sentences given, one of whom was raided only days after being released).

The arrested were said to be "charming" though they had "annoyed their neighbours" by feeding the pigeons (we are not making this up) but they had started a bomb factory in the flat — "I had no idea they were doing anything so fiendish," their actress landlady is reported as saying. ("Bomb factory" can mean, of course, weedkiller in the garden shed and sugar in the pantry).

"Security forces were put on alert for a possible bomb emergency (Standard) though a word of truth slipped out in the Guardian — "Scotland Yard said last night that there was no suggestion that the couple had any connections with the IRA or any other terrorist organisation."

Later Dafydd Ladd, only recently released from prison, was also arrested, and they were all charged with "conspiracy to cause explosions." The mystery was what explosions? Nothing had happened, nothing was about to happen, and no targets were named or suggested. Explained Insp. Bradbury in court, "we nipped the bomb-making plan in the bud," and anyway there were armed robbery charges hovering around. So far no evidence has been, or needs to be, produced, as they have not yet been committed for trial and it needs the fiat of the Attorney General — who we feel on the showing may need some convincing. However the "emergency" was reflected in exceptional security measures.

Ronan and Dafydd appear in court in handcuffs each week, Iris is in solitary confinement throughout the week (in a men's prison, the one woman), all have up to the time of writing been denied visits, all are taken to court with a police escort that exceeds that given to the I.R.A., the Kray and Messina brothers and the Angry Brigade put together. Anyone knowing how gentle and kind Iris will be staggered to see the special attention given to her at Lambeth Court.

Until some intelligible charges are made we are unable to satisfy curiosity as to "what's it all about". The raids on comrades' houses everywhere have been only for things like address books and photo albums. When police chase armed robbers they look for guns, ammunition and above all loot. There is the smell of something in the air. It would not be the first major repression, some of them involving mass slaughter, to begin as broad farce.

Tuesday 6th June. Scotland Ya.. PTA Squad, local CID, and explosive Shutter dogs raid a house in Honley, search house and question a man and a woman for three hours. Questions about their politics, local anarchists, friends who live in the area, demos attended, when and where they lived in the past, how they met Ronan and Iris and the whereabouts of G. Rua were asked. Fingerprints were taken..

Wednesday 7th June. Police go round to anarchists house at 8.30 a.m. He is at work, local CID arrive at his work place at 10 a.m. (no-one told them where he worked). They asked him to go to the police station. He was told that if he refused other ways would be found. On the way to the station he was told that Ronan had murdered a policeman a few years ago and the fact that he had won the case in court was immaterial. He was questioned for three hours at Huddersfield police station about his personal politics, what he knew about Iris and Ronan, Phil Ruff, Albert Meltzer, Stuart Christie and Graham Rua. Fingerprints were taken.

Thursday 8th June. PTA Squad visit a couple who formerly lived in the house occupied by the couple above. Similar questions are asked. They also visit the people living next door to their present address who have no personal or political connections with Ronan and Iris. And they questioned and fingerprinted a couple who live in Huddersfield (no details known).

In the first raid photographs were shown that prove that a former mailing address for Black Flag was under surveillance for some time. There was also a list of descriptions of visitors to the address. It was also obvious that the local anarchist group was under surveillance. The stress in the first two interviews was on the personal politics of the people being interviewed. At the interview of the second comrade his 'true British spirit' was appealed to and he was told that certain key helpers of the ABC were 'in the pay of Moscow.'

* * * * *

To date 6 comrades have been arrested and charged with "conspiracy to cause explosions": Iris Mills, Ronan Bennett, Dafydd Ladd, Stuart Carr, Trevor Dalton and Vince Stevenson.

1678 — 1978
TERCENTARY of the TITUS OATES PAPIST CONSPIRACY

6

Persons Unknown update (*Black Flag* V, no. 5, c. June–July 1978)

77

The months ahead contained numerous demonstrations and pickets, regular public meetings and socials, as well as events elsewhere in the country held in solidarity and to raise funds.[5] A gig took place at Conway Hall on 11 May with Crass, Poison Girls, and Charge; a Grand Anarchist Summer Ball was staged at the Metropolitan Warehouse, Wapping, on 14 August; then Crass and Poison Girls returned to Conway Hall with The Rondos on 8 September. Preceded by three hours of Q&A with the trial defendants, the show concluded with a brawl between some combination of National Front or British Movement members, Red Action or Socialist Worker Party activists, football-supporting skinheads, and general gig-goers. The police cleared the hall and among the injured was one of the beneficiaries of the gig, Vince Stevenson, who wound up in hospital with a head wound.

Expectations for the trial—reasonable given the behaviour of the prosecution—were that this would be a bitterly fought battle, requiring substantial outlay, against an establishment determined to secure a conviction. The trial date slipped from 3 September 1979 to 17 and then 20 September. And, to everyone's surprise, sixty-one days later it was all over with the defendants declared innocent on 19 December after two days of jury deliberations. The judge was so incensed at the jury that he ordered them back to the court for Carr's sentencing the following day so he could read them Carr's 'confession' and berate them. Ladd had already skipped bail, missing the verdict, and would remain in hiding until 1982 when, at a hearing on 7 June, he was freed.

Such rapid success left Persons Unknown flush with cash that was no longer required. At a press conference the day after the verdict, Bennett and Mills already suggested that the funds should be used to create a dedicated anarchist centre with *Black Flag* explaining, "There has, in fact, not been one in this country since we had to close down the old centre at Haverstock Hill." But they grudgingly added, "(apart from the Centro Iberico squat in Notting Hill)."[6]

WHO ARE THE REAL CONSPIRATORS?

In the "Persons Unknown" conspiracy case — to which we refer on another page — a blanket of silence has surrounded the charges which are being swapped around all the time. Many of our friends have been bewildered by the events and asked for an explanation which nobody outside the police (or at least, a sinister section of it) has been able to give.

We are able now to expose the bizarre truth behind the alleged conspiracy to cause explosions that never existed outside the minds of the "Anti" Terrorist Squad or which (as Insp. Bradbury said in court) were "unfortunately — I mean fortunately" prevented by too early an arrest.

There have been no terrorist-type crimes in England, or anything which could conceivably have been described as such, within the last five years other than specifically I.R.A. or Arab nationalist attacks, the perpetrators of which have been clearly defined, or the attacks made by fascist organisations upon leftist premises and persons, which the Anti-Terrorist Squad have previously denied was their responsibility and on which the police force as a whole have not acted.

It may seem incredible but it seems the Anti-Terrorist Squad were contemplating trying the trick of the Italian secret police in the case of Valpreda. Certain elements thought it would get the fascists off the hook if they could pin the blame for these fascist attacks upon anarchists. The lies and political contortions of the prostitute press make it certain that a large part of the public would be conditioned to accept automatically that libertarian socialists would be capable of any crime. The absence of motive doesn't matter when they're the dreaded anarchists!

Iris Mills (Black Box Photos)

These attacks include the bomb at the Conservative Party headquarters (proved long since to be an obvious dummy and a harmless hoax and probably for publicity) the burning down of the Socialist Workers Party headquarters by fascist elements, the arson and damage done to various trade union and Communist Party premises, the parcel bomb at Peace News, and maybe other attacks of a racial nature (though these have not been mentioned by the police) might have been brought in.

The political police, Special Branch, did not agree with this line. Politically wiser they refused to give support to the "Anti" Terrorist squad in such a frame-up. Individual statements by SB officers in private suggests that they are highly embarrassed by the antics of the brute-force and ignorance squad. But the case has already gone forward to the courts. To save face, certain charges are quietly being dropped and other more plausible ones substituted, like robberies which apparently no-one saw happening. On this we can't comment. But who are the conspirators moving in secret, who tried to get the fascists off the hook, who are part and parcel of the effective government of this country? While MPs and bishops protest against racialism, has the National Front walked into the halls of government — in classical fascist fashion — by the back door?

This is not to play at 'cops and robbers' despite the detractors. It is part of a 'game' of Anarchists and Fascists that has been going on now for sixty years, a 'game' that is being played by the so-called security services everywhere and a 'game' in which no holds are barred on their side.

Who Are the Real Conspirators? (*Black Flag* 5, no. 7, December 1978)

Persons Unknown benefit, North London Polytechnic, 11 January 1979 (Courtesy of Michael Clarke)

<u>POLICE CONSPIRACY AGAINST ANARCHISTS</u>

While Asians are being murdered on the streets by NF supporters and the Anti-Nazi League and Peace News offices have been fire-bombed by right-wingers, the Anti-Terrorist Squad is hounding and persecuting anarchists, who they say are part of a 'nation-wide conspiracy to overthrow society'. While no-one has been arrested in connection with the right-wing fire bombs, left-wing and anarchist homes have been raided by the ATS in search of evidence of just such a 'conspiracy'. The raids took place mainly in London but also across the country in Huddersfield, South Wales and Bristol.

This comes at a time when questions have been asked in the House of Commons about the role and work of the ATS and the amount spent on national defence and the police force. The ATS are concerned to show that they are doing work necessary for 'national security' and, with help from the national press, have tried to build up a theory of a Baader-Meinhof type gang of 'terrorists' who had planned to cause explosions with 'persons unknown'. As we have seen, no explosions have occurred except <u>against</u> the left.
<u>WHAT'S HAPPENING NOW</u>

The anarchists arrested, Iris Mills, Ronan Bennett, Taff Ladd, Vince Stevenson, Trevor Dawton, had been held in Brixton jail for many months.

Trevor Dawton was granted bail on 28th September. Iris Mills was given bail on 26th October. On the 11th December Vince Stevenson was granted bail. Ronan Bennett and Taff Ladd have been refused bail and will now remain in Brixton until the trial comes up, probably in 1980!

Since the time of the initial arrests, the main charge of 'Conspiracy to Cause Explosions' was dropped in November. This very serious charge meant that the defendants were all held as Category 'A' (top-security) prisoners. It also influenced the magistrates when considering bail applications.

The hysteria generated by the police via the media, is felt at the weekly court appearances. The defendants initially appeared in handcuffs and armed police patrol the court, inside and out. Harassment of Support Group members has gone on continuously.

For Iris, conditions were even worse than for the men as she was kept in a men-only prison (Brixton) for five months, as the police insisted she was 'too dangerous' for Holloway. She had spent the five months in virtual solitary confinement.
<u>NEW CHARGE</u>

The police, having failed to convince the Home Office that the defendants are a gang of dangerous 'terrorists' were forced to drop the charge and a lesser charge of 'Conspiracy to Rob' has been substituted. How long will it be before that charge is also dropped! The fact that the arrests took place and the defendants have been held, has enabled the ATS to raid, harass and intimidate the libertarian left and to gather information on the left. The <u>police conspiracy</u> of a 'terror gang' having failed, we must all give as much support as possible to the defendants so that, although three are out on bail, the case will not be forgotten.
<u>SHOW YOUR SOLIDARITY:</u> Meet outside Brixton prison on Sat. 13th January at 12 noon to picket in support of the anarchists.

SAT 21st OCTOBER
RAPED PLUS
RUDI PLUS
A.U.M. BAND
"CENTRO IBERICO"
421 Harrow Road W.9
(Westbourne Park Tube)
BENEFIT FOR PERSONS
UNKNOWN
£1.00   8 till Late

SOUNDS OCT 21

RAPED
RUDI
+ A.U.M BAND
Saturday October 21st
Centro Iberico
421A Harrow Road, W9
(Westbourne Park Tube)
BENEFIT FOR PERSONS UNKNOWN

NME OCT 21

Among the earliest
Persons Unknown
benefit gigs: Centro
Iberico (Courtesy of
Brian Young)

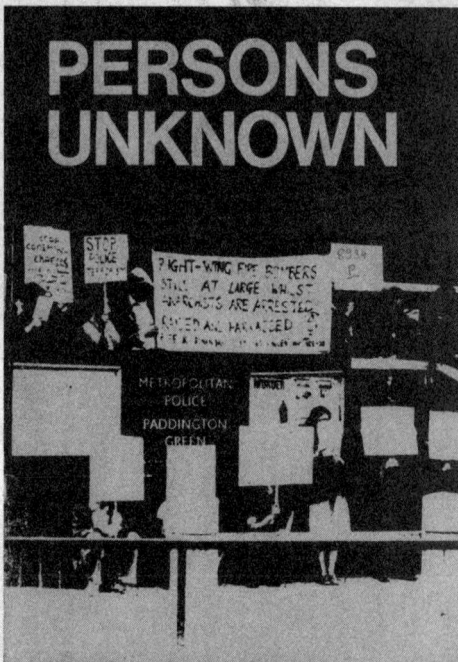

Persons Unknown pamphlet
(16 August 1979)

Anti-terrorist squad swoops on house
BOMB CACHE
SEIZED IN
LONDON RAID

Anarchist
cell hit
in Yard
arms raid

Arsenal

The men in iron masks

Bomb charge man 'an idealist'

Press exaggeration and Anti-Terror
Squad propaganda (16 August 1979)

anarchist fortnightly

Freedom

8 September / 79
Vol 40 No 16

20p

Conspiracy to Rig

Things have moved on quite a bit in the Persons Unknown case. (see Review Section). Best bit of news is that at the pretrial review on August 16th, Ronan was finally given bail. He's fine, though a bit drawn and thin.

The clumsy frame-up continues on its unsavoury way. As is now widely known the police have obtained permission to 'vet' the potential jurors. (see review for details). Not content with the weight of the bias in their favour, the prosecution are impeding the defence still further. Apparently, with only the resources of the Special Branch, The Criminal Records Office and the CID, coupled with unlimited right of challenge, they still feel a little insecure. After all the defence will have the aid of a private detective and no less than three challenges. Still, it must help to have a two week lead, before the defence get the jury list.

Rigging of juries is too much for liberal opinion, which had managed not to notice the case so far. Newspaper reports have appeared, disapproving letters have been printed in the Guardian, the NCCL has spoken up and Questions Have Been Asked In The House.

Additional complications have arisen because the Legal Aid authorities are balking at paying for the detective, so there have had to be further court hearings. The judge in question has been concerned about the way things said in "private" hearings seems to get about outside. However, he has now been convinced that "in chambers" is not the same as "in camera"(really). So our intention to reprint a few fatuous remarks no longer carries the risk of prosecution for contempt. However, we would like to reassure them all that our contempt is in no way diminished.

Were you aware that most of the adult male population of London has criminal associates? This is why this jury must be vetted. (we are not sure why the simpler approach of having a female jury was not adopted)

Anyway, with one thing and another, the court recognised today (11th) that the defence might be having a few problems, and as we said above, the Legal Aid people are a bit worried about those detective bills. Accordingly, the police are to share their information. They have graciously agreed to provide "relevant" information. And to give the defence a fair chance (after all, this is Britain) the trial has been put back again. It is now three days later, on Sept. 20

BLOOD AT THE CONWAY

Conway Hall was splashed with blood on on Saturday night as members of the British Movement tried to break up the Persons Unknown Benefit. About thirty of them gathered in the balcony, determined to stop "Crass" the anarchist band from playing. From early in the evening it was obvious that there would be nastiness. Tension built steadily. Eventually somebody realised that it was foolish to be selling bottles of beer over the bar. There were a number of skirmishes, then the real trouble broke out at about 10.30. In a series of scuffles several people were hurt, some needing to go to hospital for stitches. Scalp wounds bleed nastily. From the look of the floor, someone had bled to death.

A group of British Movement members have been specialising in this kind of thing. Their most famous exploit has been the destroying of the "Sham 69" concert at the Rainbow. Of course, this more glamorous activity has not caused them to neglect their steady work of harrassing blacks, gays etc. The British Movement has been gaining strength lately, at the expense of the National Front, which has flirted with respectability. They have, if anything, even less political ideas. At this benefit, they could have done more damage as a bloc. However, they got involved in fights in threes and fours. All bad enough, but they were contained to some extent. Later, the police arrived and turned everybody out.

The poor liberal Guardian reporter who happened to be there was horrified and wrote a totally muddled piece on it. Ironic that this appeared just next to an analysis of right wing terrorists which said that 'the attitude of the anti-terrorist squad is that it is a "detective machine, not a preventive machine'"What was all that talk last June about anarchist conspiracies being "nipped in the blood"? Still the Guardian piece had a nice photo of what appeared to be a procession of police with Union Jacks, captioned, "The right on the march"

The lesson of Saturday's incident is obvious. If you are holding a public event then you have to prepared f or trouble. On the bad side, these people succeeded in disrupting the Benefit (Crass didn't get to play). On the good side, a lot of money was raised.

It is also worth noting that the management of Conway Hall continues to insist on "free speech". They recently hired the Hall to the National Front, for a "Rock Against Commies" event.

PRE-TRIAL EVENTS

Please note new times.
Saturday Sept. 15 3.00pm. Public Meeting at Conway Hall, Following at 7.00 a Social at the Roebuck, Tottenham Court Road.

Thursday Sept. 20 Picket for first day of trial. Old Bailey

WHAT WE WANT IS MORE WORK AND LESS OF IT!

RIGHT TO WORK

Conspiracy to Rig (*Freedom* 40, no. 16, 8 September 1979)

'P.U.' CHRONOLOGY

I knew girl at 'bomb' flat—actress

24 May 78: Iris Mills & Ronan Bennett picked up in a raid on their flat.

25 May: Press reports concerning "BOMB FACTORY FLAT" etc.

27 may: Police hunt for car "FULL OF BOMBS supposedly "BOOBY TRAPPED". Iris & Ronan appear at Marleybone Magistrates Court charged with ' conspiracy to cause explosions'.

2 June: Raid on hose in North London, Taff arrested.

3 June: 'wanted' car found dumped over a cliff in Wales.

5 June: Taff Ladd with Iris & Ronan appear at Marleybone Court. All refused Bail and remanded in custody - the they protest at being hancuffed - Iris protests at being kept in solitary.

8 June: First Remand hearing at Lambeth Court - more secure. Armed police Armed police guard the court inside and out.

21 June: First news of Stewart Carr also charged with the others of 'conspiracy to cause explosions'.

4 July: Vince Stevenson picked up.

7 July: Press reports "ANARCHIST CELL HIT IN ARMS RAID". Trevor Dawton arrested. Arms & ammunition found on a raid in North London.

10 July: Vince & Trevor appear in court charged with 'conspiracy to cause explosions'.

13 July: Remand hearing at Lambeth. They protest about Iris's conditions - conditions - Ronan shouts "we are your dissidents". They are dragged from the dock and beaten up, then brought back one by one.

MORNING STAR June 6 1978

BOMB CASE 3 DRAGGED FROM DOCK

JUNE/JULY: 80 raids up and down the country.

15 August: Brixton prison, where the defentants are being held, visits are cancelled in an extensive search for a gun - none is found.

24 August: Even stricter security conditions at Lambeth court. Two members of the support group arrested and held under the Prevention of Terrorism Act for what turns out to be one small unpaid fine.

19/20 September: Numerous identity parades held. These parades fail to give grounds for adding "further serious charges" that the police claimed.

28 September: Trevor granted bail Sureties of £10,000, curfew and daily reporting.

16 November: 'Conspiracy to cause explosions' charge dropped.

23 November: 'Conspiracy to rob' charge substituted.

Chronology of Persons Unknown (*Black Flag* 5, no. 10, October 1979)

THE MILLS/BENNETT GROUP OF ANARCHISTS

Following their arrest in May and June 1978 the MILLS/
BENNETT group of anarchists appeared at the Central Criminal
Court on 20th September. Four members, Ronan BENNETT, Iris
MILLS, Trevor DAWTON and Vince STEVENSON pleaded not guilty,
Stewart CARR pleaded guilty, and Dafydd LADD failed to appear.
Following lengthy and controversial debates regarding the
vetting of the jury the trial finally began on 24th September.

The prosecution's case was based on allegations of
robberies committed by the group in order to finance and equip
future activity and the possession of loaded firearms, maps
of installations, false documents, and other apparatus of
robbery, including wigs and C.S. gas.

The jury returned on 19th December and delivered their
controversial verdict of 'Not Guilty'. The following day the
jury were ordered to return to the court to hear the case
against CARR. After sentencing him to nine years imprisonment

Judge King Hamilton extraordinarily criticised the jury's
previous decision and stirred up much public controversy
thereby.

The Mills/Bennett anarchists (Special Branch Annual Report, 1979)

TROTSKYIST AND ANARCHIST MATTERS

Persons Unknown

18. After the arrest in June of last year of Iris MILLS and Ronan
BENNETT for conspiracy with other 'persons unknown' to cause explosions
the inevitable Defence Committee was formed by radicals willing to
support such causes who referred to themselves as 'Persons Unknown'
(PUNK).

19. PUNK is a gathering of anarchists, libertarians and others,
some of whom are drawn from organisations such as Black Cross, Black
Aid, the Rising Free Collective, Justice Against the Identification
Laws (JAIL) and the Preservation of the Rights of Prisoners (PROP).
Their aim is to publicise the forthcoming trial, secure the release
of those persons concerned with this case not granted bail and to
conduct a campaign against the provisions of the Prevention of
Terrorism Act, police harassment and the ill-treatment of persons
in prison. To this end the more committed members hold regular
meetings to discuss fund-raising activities, leafleting and picketing.
Their campaign has so far, however, found little support and some
funds derived from benefit concerts have been mis-spent. As the
trial date approaches the group can be expected to increase their
activity and with the support of groups sympathetic to their cause,
hold demonstrations in the London area.

PUNK Conspiracy (Special Branch Annual Report, 1979)

TROTSKYIST AND ANARCHIST MATTERS

Trial of Six Anarchists

6. The trial began at the Central Criminal Court on 20th September of six anarchists on charges of conspiracy to rob and associated offences. The first day of the tr 1, which is expected to last for up to 2 months, was marked by the failure of one of the defendants, Daffyd LADD, to answer his bail. 'e had previously served a term of imprisonment for a serious offence of a similar nature.

Persons Unknown Benefit Concert

7. The Persons Unknown Support Group held a rock concert at the Conway Hall, Red Lion Square, WC1, on 8th September in order to raise money for the anarchists currently on trial at the Central Criminal Court. The price of admission was £1 although, in accordance with the teachings of Karl Marx people with less than £1 paid according to their ability to do so. Despite attempts by the organisers to prevent troublemakers from entering the hall a group from the British Movement managed to do so and tension grew during the evening until, at about 10 pm, fighting broke out. Police were called but as the crowd quickly dispersed no arrests were necessary.

Karl Marx: well known for his views on gig pricing (Special Branch Annual Report, 1979)

TROTSKYIST & ANARCHIST MATTERS

Four Anarchists acquitted on conspiracy charges

5. On 20th December, after a trial lasting 61 days, four anarchists, Ronan BENNETT, Iris MILLS, Trevor DAWTON and Vince STEVENSON, were acquitted by a jury at the Central Criminal Court of charges including conspiracy to rob. However, in sentencing a fifth conspirator, Stewart CARR, who had pleaded guilty, Judge King Hamilton stated that in his opinion the jury had failed to convict the other defendants on "undisputed evidence which could not confuse a child". CARR was sent to prison for nine years.

6. At a press conference after the acquittals BENNETT and MILLS, still enthusiastic for the anarchist cause, stated that they planned to open a new anarchist centre in London. When asked if he believed in violence in pursuit of his beliefs, BENNETT, after some consideration, stated that the problem was not anarchist violence but rather violence perpetrated by the State in order to bolster the capitalist system.

"… evidence which could not confuse a child" (Special Branch Annual Report, 1979)

OPTIMISM AND AUTONOMY

Crass and Poison Girls agreed to release a benefit single in support of the proposed anarchist centre. Neither the bands nor Southern Records would charge for recording, while Rough Trade would distribute it at cost meaning that—other than the record shops' cut—all profit went to the cause.

> **Penny Rimbaud:** Because we had guaranteed large sales, the best way of making real money at the time was doing a single. We agreed to fund the anarchist centre on the condition that we were not seen as proprietors and that we were not involving ourselves in how it came to work. We had a large following who would have dominated and made it one-sided—we didn't want it to become the 'Crass hide-hole.' Also, the old school anarchists, and I'd respectfully include Ronan and his mates, wouldn't have had a part to play if it had just become a punk gig centre, which it would have been if our name was attached.

Recorded over 9–10 February and released in May, *Freedom* was able to report a runaway success after just a single week: "20,000 copies … have already been snapped up in five days and a further pressing of 20,000 is underway."[1] This success came despite police intimidation with officers paying a visit to the printer preparing the single's cover, departing with the snide remark: "You need money to make bombs, don't you?" HMV stores, meanwhile, ordered their stock of the single destroyed in fear of the threatened blasphemy charges that had greeted shops selling Crass's first single.[2] Bennett himself was arrested

ANARCHIST CENTRE

Where can you meet Black
Flaggers, The Freedom Group,
The Rising Free Collective,
The Anarchy group and others
of a similar ilk over a pint
and discuss the merits and
demerits of dialectical
materialism or bourgeois
recuperation?

Where can you spend an
evening listening to some
good music without getting
ripped off by some
profiteering promoter in
the process?

Where can you hold
meetings for your group
without paying enormous
rents?

Where can you meet
people as a springboard
for other campaigns?

Well, at the moment
the answer is nowhere, but
that situation could change
very soon. A group has been
formed whose aim is to set
up an anarchist centre in
London. So far we have had
a good response from
anarchists throughout the
country and have been
successful in raising some
of the money which will be
needed for the project.

In addition to this
CRASS and POISON GIRLS, the
punk rock bands, have
recorded a single (Bloody
Revolutions/Persons Unknown)
which will be on sale
shortly. The profits from
this single will go towards
the centre and will, we hope,
go a long way in helping us
realise the scheme.

How can you help?

If you are interested in
helping set up the centre you
can:

1. Come along to the next
meeting at Conway Hall on the 6th
March at 7 p.m. (Or after that
on the 20th).
2. You can take out your
membership now. This will
guarantee you membership of the
centre for one year from the day
it opens. Membership is £15 for
those inside the London postcode
and £10 for those outside.

What will £15 get you?

£15 will get you full
membership of the centre for one
year. You will be entitled to
make use of all the centre's
facilities. These will include,
it is hoped, a bar, reading room/
library, offices, concerts. It
will also give you a say in what
the centre will be used for.

What are the aims of the
centre?

The centre has two aims:
a political one and a social one.

Our political aim is to make
anarchist ideas and literature
more easily available. We
hope that a centre will not
only be a focal point for
different anarchist groups
but also for those who are not
committed anarchists.

Our social aim is to
provide a meeting place where
people can get together and
enjoy themselves among comrades.

If you are interested......

in making contact with us
then you can either come along
to our next meeting or write to
'Anarchist Centre', C/O Freedom
Press, Angel Alley, 84b
Whitechapel High Street,
London, E1.

First announcement of the Anarchist Centre (*Black Flag* VI, no. 1, March 1980)

Anarchist centre

The idea of setting up a centre
in London where anarchists and
libertarians can meet socially as
well as politically to further anarchist ideas has met with great interest,
since last reported in Freedom
(March 15). Several hundred pounds
in donation and subscriptions have
already been raised and several
thousands are on their way from the
proceeds of the joint single released
last week by Crass and Poison Girls.
20,000 copies of the single have already been snapped up in 5 days and
a further pressing of 20,000 is underway. "Crass" and "Poison Girls"
are to be congratulated on their efforts in producing a single whose message is explicitly anarchist. The
cover (which opens out to reveal
the Queen, Pope, the Statue of Liberty and Margeret Thatcher dressed
as young punks) makes interesting
reading: in addition to mentioning
that the proceeds of the record
are to go to the anarchist centre,
the background to the Person Unknown trial is given. "Poison Girls"
contribution aptly entitled 'Persons
Unknown' makes the connection:
"We are all Unknown Persons, not
only to the authorities, but to each
other." Also:" Isolated and separa-
ted it is easier for the authorities
to pick each of us off and turn us
against each other." The tune struck
me as monotonous, but the lyrics
more than conpensate. Crass's contribution on the other side "Bloody
Revolutions" is musically more
varied (if you like punk rock), making the simple, direct statement:
"Government is government and
government is force, left or right,
or right or left, it takes the same
old course" finishing with "nothing
is really different, 'cos all governments the same, they can call it
freedom but slavery is the game,
there is nothing that you offer, but

a dream of last year's hero, the
truth of revolution, brother ....is
year zero." Exactly.

The thought of it reaching no1
in the charts is intriguing I
wonder how 'Top of the Pops'would
handle that.

Meanwhile the search of suitable
premises for the centre, (which it
has been suggested might be called
the "Autonomy Club") continues
and a sympathetic architect has
offered to make surveys to ensure
that the building complies with
building regulation and safety standards. If anyone knows of potentially suitable premises, perhaps he/
she could write to Anarchist Centre
c/o 84b Whitechapel High St., London. And if you want to help in
setting up the anarchist centre come
along to the next meeting on Thurs.
19th June 7.30pm at Conway Hall.

Crass, Poison Girls, and the Autonomy Club (*Freedom* 41, no. 10, 24 May 1980)

and held in custody at Epping police station while on his way to meet Crass. Suspicions remain that the phone used to confirm his visit was tapped as he was picked up while waiting for his lift at the exact time he had given on the call.

The liner notes to the 7" closely reflected a press piece used in *Freedom* and *Black Flag*. It spoke of creating a space, comparable to the numerous political clubs on the continent, where like-minded individuals could socialise, make connections, find literature, and attend events.

> **Kay Byatt:** When people started talking about the anarchy centre the scene had really kicked off, so anyone who did a gig, the money was to go toward the centre. We'd get friends to copy flyers at work, bump into people and tell them where there was a gig on. Nobody ever made any money or took any money, so it'd be a quid to get in and it was all for the centre. We were all thinking, "Yeah, this is a centre for us!" so we were very happy supporting it.

For a time, the 'anarchy centre' group was undoubtedly the wealthiest anarchist collective in the entire country, with £3,200 banked by August and £4,500 by November. At a Conway Hall meeting on 11 December, the organisers declared that £3,000 had so far come from the 7", with more to come, and more moderate sums coming from subscriptions (a year for £15 or £10 for those outside of London or overseas), donations, and regular fundraisers. It is an unanswered question of how much of the funding pool was money left over from the trial, if any.

The organisers' ambition was on display in their request that supporters look for properties of around fifteen thousand square feet with several side rooms. A property on Farringdon Road was investigated but declined. Someone also suggested at a public meeting "that the Centro Iberico in Harrow Road should be approached with a view to mounting Anarchist Centre meetings, gigs, etc.... As there is already a large building squatted by anarchists, it would be a good idea to make use of it."[3] Ultimately, the 01 Warehouse, Metropolitan Wharf, Wapping, was selected.

ANARCHIST CENTRE

PLANS FOR THE ANARCHIST CENTRE ARE RAPIDLY COMING TO MAT-
URITY. SO FAR MORE THAN £500 HAS BEEN RAISED THROUGH
SUBSCRIPTIONS. MORE THAN 100 PEOPLE HAVE PAID FULL OR
PART SUBSCRIPTIONS FOR MEMBERSHIP. THE RECORD "BLOODY
REVOLUTIONS & PERSONS UNKNOWN" BY CRASS & POISON GIRL
WILL BE ON SALE BY THE TIME THIS ISSUE IS OUT. THE PROF-
ITS FROM THIS RECORD ARE GOING TOWARDS THE ESTABLISHMENT
OF AN ANARCHIST CENTRE IN LONDON. ONCE WE HAVE THAT
MONEY WE CAN BEGIN IN EARNEST TO FIND SUITABLE PREMISES.

WITH A SUITABLE PERMANENT BASE, WHERE ANARCHISTS FROM
ENGLAND AND COMRADES FROM OVERSEAS CAN MEET, WE HOPE
THAT THE ANARCHIST MOVEMENT WILL GROW STRONGER AND MORE
COHESIVE. PERHAPS IT WILL THE BEGINNING OF A NETWORK OF
SIMILAR CLUBS.

MEETINGS: CONWAY HALL, 25 RED LION SQUARE, HOLBORN, WC1.

THURSDAY 22ND MAY; THURSDAY 19TH JUNE.

SINCE WE ADVERTISED THE IDEA OF AN ANARCHIST CENTRE IN
THE LAST BLACK FLAG & FREEDOM A GREAT DEAL OF INTEREST
HAS BEEN SHOWN. IF YOU WANT TO BE INVOLVED..YOU CAN...
COME ALONG TO ONE OF THE MEETINGS..OR SUBSCRIBE NOW.
WRITE TO: ANARCHIST CENTRE, C/O FREEDOM BOOKSHOP, 84B
         WHITECHAPEL HIGH STREET, LONDON E1.

THE CRASS/POISON GIRLS
SINGLE IS NOW ON SALE.
BUY IT. PROFITS TO THE
ANARCHIST CENTRE.
BLOODY REVOLUTIONS /
PERSONS UNKNOWN ...70P.

PRICE CHANGE.
THE PRICE OF BLACK FLAG
WILL BE 25PENCE FROM THE
NEXT ISSUE. WE REGRET
HAVING TO INCREASE THE
PRICE BUT THE INCREASES
IN THE POSTAL RATES HAVE

£500 and 100 Subscriptions...
(*Black Flag* VI, no. 2, June 1980)

THE forces of law and order are showing an intense interest in the musical output of the anarchist band, Crass, these days. At the moment, three of Crass' records are under threat, either for blasphemy and/or obscenity or because the record sleeve of their latest joint single with Poison Girls - "Bloody Revolutions"/"Persons Unknown" - might cause offence to their majesties, the Queen, the Prime Minister, the Pope or the Statue of Liberty for being portrayed as punks propping up a wall in a dingy back alley.

A couple of months ago police in Birmingham called in to a couple of record shops and told the proprietors not to sell any Crass records. The manager of one of the shops, Towering Inferno, said that the police warned him that the Director of Public Prosecutions thought the records, "Shaved Woman"/"Reality Asylum" and "The Feeding of the Five Thousand" were blasphemous and if he continued to sell them his stock would be seized.

Crass, however, say they have a letter from Scotland Yard saying there will be no charges of blasphemy. Both shops have continued to sell the records in question without any further police hassles.

Blasphemy and obscenity (*Freedom* 41, no. 12, 21st June 1980)

Little A Press, a radical printer, was based in the same building and it had hosted the Anarchist Summer Ball in 1979. Renovations started in June 1981 and concluded in August.

On 6 June, *Freedom* published updated finances stating that the funding pool stood at £4,200. Building materials to convert the warehouse were estimated at £1,500 and a year of rent and rates at £3,100.[4] The centre was viable given it would only need £400—plus a sum for coffee, tea, and sundries—to survive a full year, during which it could expect further subscriptions, donations and fundraisers as well as revenue from the single. Sources quote £10,000 raised by the single which is not unreasonable given that 50p per copy, at a time when singles cost £1 or more, should have seen that figure reached just from the first pressing of twenty thousand.

Wapping, at the time, was a liminal space hovering between an industrial past and an unknown future. Ghosts loomed in the form of abandoned wharves, deteriorating storage depots, battered cobblestones bare of traffic, and ranks of empty warehouses. Tony Drayton believes the choice of location was an obvious error: "It should never have been there! It was so cut off, there was no commercial sense to it at all. You would never go to Wapping if you didn't have a reason. There was no reason to be passing by, no passing trade at all. It was totally unwelcoming."

> **Ruth Doll (Hagar the Womb):** It really did feel like we were dropped into another era every Sunday night: it was all mists and empty cobbled streets, very Dickensian. We barely encountered a soul either on the way to or from Wapping station, or in the building itself, it felt like nothing stirred in that part of London except us. I'm sure our antics were noticed, there were complaints, but we didn't see anyone let alone anyone pissed off with us!

> **Penny Rimbaud:** It was genuinely Dickensian: it hadn't been touched since that era. The whole place stunk of herbs and spices.

Money for Bombs

The Crass/Poison Girls single 'Bloody Revolutions/Persons Unknown' is causing a bit of bovver. Recently paying a visit to the printer who did the cover, the police confiscated a 'sample' copy and as they were leaving said, "You need money to make bombs, don't you". We always thought that flour, sugar and weedkiller were the classic ingredients!

Meanwhile HMV, the record chain store, have ordered that all their stocks of the single, which is gradually creeping towards the Top 50, be destroyed as they are worried that police harrassment against the record shops around the country may be directed against them, too.

Crass' previous single, 'Reality Asylum/Shaved Women', about Christ and collaborators respectively, had its unfair share of hassles as well, with the Vice Squad threatening to do the group for blasphemy. The DPP decided not to proceed in that instance but recently some record shops holding the single were told by the police that the record was "damaging to the morals of those under 18" and by selling it could be committing an offence. As we experienced with an earlier issue of Black Flag, satire can cause offence quite easily.

Profits from 'Bloody/Revolutions/Persons Unknown' (U.K. price 70p) go to the forthcoming Anarchist Centre. If you want to get hold of a copy or any of the other Crass or Poison Girls records, but can't get them through your local record dealer, the following outlets can be contacted:

ROUGH TRADE: 202 Kensington Park Road, London, W11; ROUGH TRADE: 1412 Grant Avenue, San Francisco, California 94133; ZENSOR: Belzigerstrasse 23, 1 Berlin 30; GIUCAR: via

Anarchist Centre

THE next meeting is at Conway Hall, Red Lion Square, London at 7.30 p.m. on Wednesday, 27 August. £3,200 has been raised so far from the first pressing of the Crass/Poison Girls single and from subscriptions and donations. Full subscriptions are £15 (London) and £10 (the rest of the world!) for a year's membership. The more people who subscribe now (any sum will be taken in instalments) the quicker the Centre will get off the ground. Write (sae please) to Anarchist Centre, c/o FREEDOM, 84b Whitechapel High St, London E1.

Crass and Poison Girls take the total to £3,200 (*Freedom* 41, no. 16, 16 August 1980)

Money to make bombs (*Black Flag* VI, no. 3, c. July–August 1980)

The name 'Autonomy Club' had been mooted as far back as May 1980 and, though it was usually referred to simply as 'the anarchist centre' for most of the next year, it was formally christened in late summer before an inaugural debate on Friday 21 August. *Freedom* began printing a monthly events listing updating people on what to expect Thursday–Friday–Saturday, the three nights a week the Autonomy Centre would be open. The schedule included a housewarming on 18 September, various films, knock-out darts, a couple of debates, literature mail-out by the A Distribution Collective every Thursday.[5]

And by the 10 October issue of *Freedom*, the Autonomy Centre was in trouble. The note placed in the paper was stark: "This month has fewer events planned than last, mainly because we're running out of ideas. Ideas, particularly money-raising ones, are desperately needed." This sense of crisis is hard to understand. If the numbers published in June were accurate then, without any further income, the refurbished centre opened with roughly £2,000 in the bank, reduced to around £1,300 when the next quarter's rent, £680 plus rates, was paid. It's also hard to see money-spinning, audience-raising genius in doing even less with the space.[6]

There's no indication that building work or furnishings ran thousands of pounds over budget, so unanswered questions remain. First, a minimum of twenty thousand copies of the single sold couldn't add up to £3,000—10p per copy—so what did it bring in? Second, what other sums of money were raised June–October? Basically, how did the centre wind up in dire straits within seven weeks?

Issues were perhaps predictable from day one. The December 1980 meeting showed attempts to estimate potential audiences starting only after the search for a sizeable venue had begun. A reliance on memberships and letters of interest, often from people neither in London nor the UK, led the anarchists to significantly overestimate attendance. Based on the June figures, even if the single had raised no more than the sum declared in December, all other fundraising fell £2,000 short of covering the costs. Without the single and the punk benefit gigs, the anarchists commanded

ANARCHIST CENTRE

JOIN!

Thanks to Crass, Poison Girls and a number of other bands, as well as the many people who've responded to our requests for money the Anarchist Centre now has in its coffers about £4,500, easily making us the wealthiest anarchist group in the country.

Be this as it may the biggest hurdle has still to be overcome – the finding of suitable premises. In the last few weeks we have looked at several likely places and have put in tenders for two of them. We cannot even guess as to how successful our tenders will be, but we should hear back from the agents soon.

The cost of obtaining such a place (not to mention its upkeep once we get it) is extremely high and we will need your support if we are to open and stay open.

In order to do a proper cost evaluation it is essential for us to know how many people are likely to use the Centre, so we would welcome not only membership fees now, but also letters from people interested in the project who would be prepared to use it, help run it, or have some skill which might be useful. We

also welcome any suggestions about what use the Centre can be put, any information about possible sites, or how we can reach more people with news of the ideas.

For those of you who are members or are on the mailing list, the October newsletter has been printed and is on its way. There was no September issue.

In the near future we intend to hold a meeting open to members and all those interested in the Anarchist Centre to discuss ways in which we can speed things up. News of this

meeting will be carried in Freedom and those on the mailing list will be notified.

For those of you who haven't already taken out membership but intend to eventually, please do it now. The more members we get the sooner we can open.

Membership: £15 for those in London, £10 for those outside.

Cheques payable to: "William Godwin Memorial Society" c/o Freedom Press, Angel Alley, 84b Whitechapel High Street, London E1.

page 2

£4,500: the wealthiest anarchist group in the country (*Black Flag* VI, no. 5, 5 November 1980)

Ⓐ CENTRE

ABOUT 35 people attended the Anarchist Centre meeting at the Conway Hall on 11 December. Ronan Bennett reported that there were about £4000 in the kitty, about £3000 of which had come from the Crass/Poison Girls record, but that the money didn't seem to be coming in as fast as before, probably because apparently nothing is happening.

Premises which might be suitable have been found in Farringdon Street (or was it Road?) but as it is a double property and the centre would only need half of it, it isn't certain whether the negotiations will be successful.

There was a long discussion about the need to involve as many people as possible in the centre, both to get it off the ground in the first place and to keep it going once it's opened. Two concrete suggestions came out of this. One, that everyone who lives in London should keep their eyes open for any property that might be suitable - warehouses, derelict churches (!) etc - ring the relevant estate agent to see if it's still available, what the floor area and other facilities are (what's wanted is a hall with at least 15,000 square feet and a

couple of other rooms besides), and then, if it sounds hopeful, to ring Ronan (leave a message at Rising Free: 01-359-3788) and give him all the details.

The second, and in the short term probably the most hopeful, suggestion was that the Centro Iberico in Harrow Road should be approached with a view to mounting Anarchist Centre meetings, gigs etc. there. The idea was that as there is already a large building squatted by anarchists, it would be a good idea to make use of it, if we can, so that the Centre can be seen to be doing something real, rather than just existing as a pipe dream in the heads of a few Utopians. There will be a meeting early in the new year to report back on the discussions with Centro Iberico. In the meantime, keep your eyes peeled and watch this space.

V.

KILNER HOUSE

ON Wednesday, 10 December Sheriff Black called at Kilner for a pre-arranged meeting to 'discuss' the eviction. He was accompanied by a policeman in a pinstripe suit. Black named Monday, 5 January as the day he expects us all to leave. We remain prepared.

S.H.

Temporary approach to Centro Iberico (*Freedom* 41, no. 25, 20 December 1980)

barely a fraction of the support needed to rent a £3,100 a year venue.

The single's liner notes had testified to a youthful desire for "somewhere to go for a drink and a cuppa … to set up a gig facility. At the moment we're looking at an old factory as a possibility so that bands that don't want to play the usual commercial circuit will have an alternative. It could mean that, at least, anarchist punks will have somewhere of their own to go." On the contrary, the organisers acquired neither a drinks license nor an entertainment license.

The problem was compounded by arrogance and hubris. In the October note, the anarchists sneered at their 'comrades': "There's now drink available at all times so there's no excuse for going to the pub instead. We're also hiring a pool table and Vince (Stevenson) will challenge anyone interested to a game any Friday." On 21 November, the same irritation with those who had made the centre possible was visible in a debate entitled 'Young People Are Over-rated?'

Based on public notices, in the twenty-four days the centre was open 20 August–10 October, there were just four paid events: 50p (members) or £1.50 (nonmembers) to attend one of three films; 30p for darts night. Otherwise, the thrills on offer were helping A Distribution post literature once a week, four or five talks or debates, two members' meetings, and a surfeit of drop-in time for a place with no passing trade. Mostly it acted as a break room for workers from Little A.

The organisers estimated costs of £50 a week—presumably a rough breakdown of the rent, rates, and expenses. This was a lot of money for a space in an insalubrious and inappropriate location, that was closed four out of every seven days. Yet the listings show that the anarchist true believers never conceived of offering events with a realistic prospect of luring a crowd to Wapping; they focused on being a political office with few concessions to entertainment.

Presumably, the belief was that revenue would be topped up by benefit events, donations through the post, and benevolence

AUTONOMY CENTRE

AFTER months of searching, suitable premises for the Autonomy Centre have been found in a warehouse in Wapping, East London. At the moment the warehouse is just a shell and some building, decorating and electrical work will need to be done before it can open.

A temporary Co-ordinating Committee has been formed in order to get the work completed as soon as possible. Then, after four months it will be up to the membership to decide on how they want the Centre to be run. So if you haven't joined already, now is the time to do it. The annual subscription rates have been reduced to £7 (waged) or £5 (unemployed). Those who have already paid the provisional full membership of £15, or anyone sending £15 before 1st June will be given life membership.

At the moment the Centre's funds stand at about £4,200, but rates and rent alone for the first year will cost £3,100. In addition the cost of building materials alone will require another £1500. That of course means we need more funds and lots of offers of free labour. Please send subscriptions/donations to Autonomy Centre, c/o Freedom, 84B Whitechapel High Street, London E1. (cheques, P.O.s made out to the William Godwin Memorial Society) If you can help with building or decorating (no skills required), please send us details of how to contact you as soon as possible.

A. F.

New Wapping home (*Freedom* 42, no. 11, 5 June 1981)

Metropolitan Wharf (Mick Slaughter, c. 1981)

ANARCHIST CENTRE

After months of searching, premises have finally been found for the Anarchist Centre. These are at: 1st Floor, O&N Warehouse, Wapping Wall, London E1.

At the moment the pre ses are being fitted out decorated. The organ rs hope to have the Centre open by July. All those who can help with the building work are urged contact the Centre throug Freedom Press, Angel Alle Whitechapel High St, London E1.

As soon as the Centre is habitable a meeting of the membership will be held discuss the future of t Centre.

There is still time to become a life member fo £15. Annual membership is £7 and £5 for the unwaged. Cheques payable to: "William Godwin Memorial Society" send c/o Freedom Press.

Fitting out (*Black Flag* VI, no. 8, July 1981)

Autonomy Centre

Months of searching for premises and weeks of building and decorating work have finally paid off — London's Autonomy Centre is now open.

The Centre has so far been financed by profits from a Crass/Poison Girls single and from donations and membership subscriptions.

When things get going, it is hoped that people will use it for conferences and meetings, as well as turning up for social events and just dropping in for a chat with whoever is around. Black Flag and A Distribution have offices at the Centre and structureless tyrants from Xtra! are members, so it will be a good place to meet these people if you want to.

For the time being, however, the Centre will be open on Thursday nights from 7pm and on Fridays and Saturdays from 2pm. A Distribution meets on alternate Thursday nights to distribute most of the UK's anarchist publications and would welcome help from anyone with time to spare. Films, debates and talks have also been arranged for some of these nights and an official opening night, with alternative cabaret comedian, Tony Allen (and friends) is planned for the end of September.

If you want to know more about the Centre, or if you want to join, write to: The Autonomy Centre, O Warehouse, Metropolitan Wharf, Wapping Wall, London E1. Membership is incredibly cheap — only £7 (£5 for the unemployed) and it entitles you to reductions to films and social events. Also donations are still needed as the Centre is costing about £50 a week to run.

If you want up to date information about events being run at the Centre, you'll find a list printed in Freedom every fortnight (on the back page). Otherwise you can call the Centre during its open hours on: 01-481 3537.

The opening of the Autonomy Centre (*Xtra* no. 9, c. August–September 1981)

at drop-in sessions; and it is true that benefits continued to be staged such as a disco at the New Inn, Moseley, on 29 October. A gig also happened at Wapping on Sunday 18 October—The Apostles, Cold War, Twelve Cubic Feet, and What Is Oil?—testing the waters for one bona fide revenue generator. Without them, showings of *The War Game*, *Pleasure at Her Majesty's*, and *Stand Up and Be Counted* would have had to attract nearly one hundred attendees each. Unless the darts and pool came to the rescue!

A fresh note entitled 'Urgent! Special Meeting to Discuss Future!' appeared. After this session on Friday 6 November, the anarchists turned, belatedly and grudgingly, to the punks. The anarchists would run the centre from Thursday to Saturday; the punks staged gigs on Sundays.

> **Tony Drayton (Kill Your Pet Puppy):** Andy Martin (of The Apostles) was working for Little A: he was the one to tell the Autonomy Centre to put on some gigs: there was no bar, no food, no reason for anyone to turn up otherwise. He was the main man at Wapping.

> **Jon Attwood (Screaming Babies and Hagar the Womb):** Chris (Knowles) was especially good at networking and got Cold War invited to play in Southend. Also playing were The Apostles who told us about the Autonomy Centre so we went the next week, then a week or two later was the first gig—a group of us went most weeks, anything from two or three to fifteen of us. We got to know Andy Martin and the Scum Collective who put on the gigs. He wasn't the stereotypical punk you would have expected and put on some of the stranger Hornchurch bands: Boiled Eggs, What Is Oil?, Screaming Babies, and the one-off noise/improv group Jim Face and the Farmers—the only qualification for being in that band was coming from Hornchurch although Andy was an honorary guest at the gig.

Not coincidentally, the November event listing was the first to mention a punk gig … and the last to appear. As at Centro

AUTONOMY CENTRE EVENTS

EVENTS FOR SEPTEMBER

Thursday 3rd: A Distribution
                  (all help welcome)
Friday 4th: Film 'The War Game'
   50p members, £1 non-members
Saturday 5th: 'Drop in' Day
Thursday 10th: A Distribution
Friday 11th: Gareth Pierce
                  (solicitor) speaks on
                  McMahon case
                  (all you wanted to know
                  about supergrasses)
Saturday 12th: Film 'Pleasure
                  at Her Majesties'
                  John Clees etc
Members £1, non-members £1.50

Meetings, debates, darts, and drop-ins
(*Freedom* event listings for the Autonomy
Centre, September–October 1981)

AUTONOMY CENTRE EVENTS

Thursday 17th: A Distribution
                   7pm
Saturday 19th: Film 'Stand
                  up and be counted'
                  about conscientious
                  objection in the IWW
                  and general strike
                   7.30 pm
         Members £1, others £1.50
Thursday 24th: A Distribution
                   7pm
Friday 25th: Debate on
                   Feminism
                   7.30pm
Saturday 26th: Members meeting
                   3pm

AUTONOMY CENTRE EVENTS

EVENTS FOR SEPTEMBER

Friday 25th: Debate on
                   Feminism
                   7.30pm
Saturday 26th: Members meeting
                   3pm

AUTONOMY CENTRE EVENTS

FOR OCTOBER 1981

Fri 9 Oct:	Debate: Is revolutionary violence ever justified?	Sat 31 Oct:	Halloween event. Live music, drink!!! £1.50 non-members, £1 members.
Sat 10 Oct:	Knock out darts, or knock out chess. 30p entrance. Genuine cash prizes!!!		
Wed 14 Oct:	Drop in between 2.30-5.30pm.		
Thurs 15 Oct:	Drop in after 7 pm.		
Fri 16 Oct:	Drop in after 2 pm.		
Sat 17 Oct:	Drop in after 6.30pm.		
Wed 21 Oct:	Drop in between 2.30-5.30pm.		
Thurs 22 Oct:	A Distribution mailout.		
Fri 23 Oct:	Drop in after 2 pm.		
Sat 24 Oct:	Drop in after 6.30pm.		
Wed 28 Oct:	Drop in between 2.30-5.30pm.		
Thurs 29 Oct:	Drop in after 7 pm.		
Fri 30 Oct:	Drop in after 2 pm.		

Notes

Last month's events met with mixed success. You came along in droves to the party, but seemed pretty unimpressed with the selection of films. Debates attracted a hard core of people hoping for blood, but drop in times were a bit bleak for the people opening up the centre. There's now drink available at all times so there's no excuse for going to the pub instead. We're also hiring a pool table and Vince will challenge anyone interested to a game any Friday. This month has fewer events planned than last, mainly because we're running out of ideas. Ideas, particularly money-raising ones are desperately needed.

Autonomy Centre
01 Warehouse
Metropolitan Wharf
Wapping Wall
London E1
Tel 481 — 3537

AUTONOMY CENTRE EVENTS

EVENTS

Saturday 24th October   7.00pm
Autonomy Centre
Two video films about Squatting
and the Recent Riots in Berlin.
Admission: 75p
and address

Fri 23 Oct:	Drop in after 2 pm.
Sat 24 Oct:	Drop in after 6.30pm.
Wed 28 Oct:	Drop in between 2.30-5.30pm.
Thurs 29 Oct:	Drop in after 7 pm.
Fri 30 Oct:	Drop in after 2 pm.
Sat 31 Oct:	Halloween event. Live music, drink!!! £1.50 non-members, £1 members.

Enjoy Halloween as never before
at the Autonomy Centre. The party starts at 8pm. on Saturday
October 31st. with live music
from 'The Helicopters' and a cabaret by Tony Allen. Food and
drink provided!

Iberico, becoming a music venue meant exclusion from the anarchist press. The last event mentioned was the Big A Sale on Saturday 12 December: an anarchist book fair and fundraiser. *Freedom* declared that the centre "desperately needs help to pay the rent and rates, which together add up to approximately £80 per week. Paying this would place an intolerable burden on the centre as all its time and space would be devoted to fundraising."[7]

More positively for the punks, having the chance to shape some part of a space they'd helped fund felt like a step forward.

> **Kay Byatt:** It had a real community hub feel, no bouncers on the door, nothing commercial. If someone had travelled all the way down for the gig and didn't have the money to get in, people would just say, "Don't worry about it." We could do what we wanted! You had people selling their fanzines, selling tapes they'd done; there was no bar so people would take their own cans or sell homebrew; there was coffee and tea so you could just sit and read if you wanted. We'd all go every Sunday, never missed anything. The area being so industrial, nothing else there, it almost made it more appealing because it was really its own thing. People would travel a long way and even crash there.

> **Phil Barker (Lack of Knowledge):** Having bought the "Bloody Revolutions" single in 1980, I'd heard about the place. I first went the Christmas that Crass played as the Shaved Women. My first impression was that it wasn't all about the music: there was a room with books, magazines, pamphlets, posters—antiwar, vegetarianism, feminism, compassion in world farming.... I was still at school so this was a new kind of education, dangerous and exciting!

> **Steve Ignorant:** There was an outside corridor, a kitchen to one side, and a few more small rooms, but the main space itself fitted about two hundred people. I'd expected there'd be a comfy corner where you could sit and maybe there'd

Autonomy Centre

WE think it is fair now to claim that London's Autonomy Centre is established and should be supported as a permanent venue for Londoners and visitors alike.

A tremendous amount of work has been put into turning an old dockside warehouse into a brightly-lit meeting place, and the comrades and friends who have contributed work and money into creating this badly-needed centre are to be warmly congratulated.

A housewarming party for members and guests on Friday, 18th September was well-attended and went off in great spirit with a real live group and Tony Allen for cabaret. A continuing programme of debates, film shows and other events is taking shape. Every alternative Thursday evening (the Thursday when FREEDOM is despatched to our readers) the A Distribution Collective, which now has its office on the premises, carries out its complicated task of despatching a wide variety of anarchist literature from many sources to bookshops around the country.

Like the A Distribution Collective, the Autonomy Centre is already bringing together individuals and groups who hitherto had little contact with each other, even though we may have been working in neighbouring areas of London. And that can't be bad.

Apart from the working party, the Centre is open on Thursday evenings — and on Fridays and Saturday evenings as well, with some activity organised, or not as the case may be.

Last Friday, 25th September, a debate on Feminism was held, proposed by Iris Mills, opposed by Carol Saunders, and followed by a lively discussion. We have been lucky enough to get the texts of the opening contributions — and feel they open up areas of argument well worth following up. Let's have your contributions on the subject of:

Housewarming, debates, films ... no gigs?
(*Freedom* 42, no. 20, 10 October 1981)

be bookshelves but what I remember is just a little stage at the end, very small, it might have been wooden pallets or something. The toilets weren't flushing either which I wound up trying to fix but couldn't.

Tony Drayton: There were no drinks available and the nearest options were quite a walk away. We did those walks and quickly found out it was best to do them in convoy for two reasons: first, safety as you had to walk into a pub ten minutes away and ask for a takeaway; second, so as not to signal that the gigs were happening. To counter this, the Puppy Collective organised bringing in crates of cans to sell at cost price.

Within two weeks of gigs starting, Brett (Puppy) decided he would bring in food to sell. One person volunteered to take over bringing in the drinks as he had a car—tremendous! We had been bringing all the crates of drink on the tube, now all we were bringing was Brett's curry, five of us with massive containers. Feeding of the 5,000 had nothing on this. The drinks and food room became as central as the bands on stage.

Lacking licenses, the organisers needed to proceed discreetly. Albert Meltzer would later write the anarchists' view of what occurred instead: "With the punks' money came the punks, and in the first week they had ripped up every single piece of furniture carefully bought, planned and fitted, down the to the lavatory fittings that had been installed by Ronan [Bennett] from scratch, and defaced our own and everyone else's walls for blocks around. In the excitement of the first gigs where they could do as they liked, they did as they liked and wrecked the place."[8]

This retrospective statement has become canon but should be treated with caution. The organisers were pleading impoverishment a month before gigs commenced and no contemporary report mentions a punk apocalypse. While it's conceivable that overexcited punks caused damage, it's less believable that

AUTONOMY CENTRE
URGENT!

SPECIAL MEETING
to discuss
FUTURE!
Friday 6 Nov 7.30pm

AUTONOMY CENTRE
01 Warehouse, Metropolitan Wharf, Wapping Wall, London E1 4LG
01 481 3557

EVENTS FOR NOVEMBER

Fri 20	Members meeting. Please come, there's lots to discuss.
Sat 21	Debate: Young people are over-rated...?
Sun 22	Gig from 7 pm with: Terminal Disaster, Cold War, Anabolic Steroids, Urban Dissidents, Flack, Assassins of Hope. Entrance to be arranged.
Wed 25	Drop in from 2.30 — 5.30 pm.
Thurs 26	Drop in after 7 pm.
Fri 27	Social event from 8 pm with JJ and the Flyers and the Bat Band. Entrance £1.25. Bar.
Wed 2 Dec	Drop in from 2.30 — 5.30 pm.
Thurs 3 Dec	A Distribution mailout from 7.30 pm. Help appreciated.
Fri 4 Dec	Talk: Peter Neville on 'The Origins of the British Police'.

CHRISTOPHER DAVIS APPRECIATION SOCIETY

Nov 26th:		Dance
Dec 3rd:		Charlotte Baggins
		'I don't want no revolution
		I can't dance to'

All events on Thursdays, 8 pm at the New Inn, Moseley Rd.

FREEDOM PARTY:
Following an ancient tradition on Sat 19th December, the Freedom Collective will be at home in the Bookshop from midday — bring plenty of drink.

From one traveller to another, best wishes, good luck.
A Flyer

AUTONOMY CENTRE — BIG A SALE

ON Saturday the 12th of December A Distribution is organising an Anarchist Book Fair at the Autonomy Centre. The groups at present taking part include: A Distribution, Freedom Press, 121 Bookshop and Pandoras Books. Ten per cent of sales will go to the Autonomy Centre. And most books will be sold at twenty-five per cent discount. Food and drink will be provided.

If there are any other groups interested in taking part could they write to the 'Anarchist Book Fair' c/o Freedom.

AND...!

FOR the Autonomy Centre to survive it desperately needs help to pay the rent and rates, which together add up to approximately £80 per week. Paying this would place an intolerable burden on the Centre as all its time and space would be devoted to fundraising.

What we need is relatively well-off comrades to support the Autonomy Centre to the tune of a quid a week. Contact us (with SAE) and we'll send a Standing Order form. If you do not want that just write and we'll arrange an alternative method. Autonomy Centre c/o Freedom.

BIG A SALE

Anarcho-Productions of Wapping bring you — The Big A Sale! Yes Folks! On Saturday, 12th December at the Autonomy Centre, Wapping, all the Anarchist Publishers will be having a sale. A massive 25%, repeat 25% off all titles now is the time to stock your bookshelves, help your local friendly Anarchist Press and support the Centre too! Don't delay — come to the Big A! You know it makes sense!

Punks start, Centre stops (*Freedom* event listings for the Autonomy Centre November–December 1981)

BIG A SALE

IN the bitter snows of winter last Saturday, the great and glorious Big A Sale took place in the Autonomy Centre at Wapping in East London. All the illustrious Anarchist printing houses were represented and proffered their wares to the panting public. Conceived in reply to the infamous Socialist Book Fair with its packs of opportunist, commercial and 'sincerely committed' leftist publishers, the Big A Sale gathered Cienfuegos, 121 Bookshop Brixton, the late Rising Free and of course Freedom (to name but many) together in order to benefit both their own and the Autonomy Centre's dwindling coffers; the A centre in particular having an imminent crisis of finance on their hands in order to pay the next 3 months rent.

But, as we all know, the inclemency of the weather last Saturday drove all but the most hardy and revolutionary of bookworms deeper into their armchairs, toasting another teacake and wiping away a tear of regret.

Open from 10am — 6pm, the poor old A centre installed a special no-heat heating system in order to preserve the books but helped refrigerate the booksellers. Freedom's stall sold a modest number of publications, but lacked the impact and variety of the juicy spreads displayed by Cienfuegos and Rising Free. Turnout was modest, but larger than expected, the weather being what it was.

Hopefully something like it will be organised again as it has great potential. An opportunity to get so much anarchist stuff in one place should not be missed and ideally should help attract the merely curious as well as the hard bitten anarch. One thing though, the world wide publicity provided by only advertising the event in FREEDOM, while extensive, is not going to get them flocking in from the likes of Neasden where FREEDOM is not a notably big seller.

AUTONOMY CENTRE DEBATE

SO far there have been three debates at the Autonomy Centre, one on feminism, one on revolutionary violence and one on young people. It seems to me that debates should be a regular feature of the Centre since they give an opportunity for ideas to be communicated and this is surely the main function of anarchism; getting our ideas across to people. Now one of the ideas of the Centre is that people don't just sit back and wait for things to happen, they go and make them happen. Since I think there ought to be debates at the Centre, it's up to me to put them on and that is why on Friday 11th December at 7.30 pm I'll be speaking in favour of the motion that 'Marx was wrong'.

The choice of subject was made for two reasons. Firstly, it is important to show Marxists that theirs is not the only type of anti-capitalism and that there exists an alternative to state socialism. Secondly, there is the fact that a lot of anarchists accept Marx's economic ideas, his concept of the class struggle. I suggest that Marx's view of the economy and the class struggle is entirely wrong and that accepting Marx's economics leads to a complete misunderstanding of how society really works. If we don't genuinely understand how the system works, we can't hope to change it.

So much for this particular debate. I intend to arrange one on a different subject for January. Hopefully there'll be at least one debate every month. Incidentally, the Trotskyist group I asked to provide someone to speak against the motion haven't replied yet so it looks as if the damage to toilets, side rooms, kitchen, and main room amounted to hundreds of pounds in chairs, shelves, walls, stage, and toilet pull chains.

> **Grant Brand (Rudimentary Peni):** Every Sunday through-out the winter of 1981, I made the journey to Wapping to work as a volunteer. We put on gigs, sold anarchist books and magazines, and used it as a venue for discussion groups. I just went up there and helped out and I wasn't paid so they didn't object. There was no significant damage during my time. I did hear they never had a music license and that caused a problem in the end.

> **Tony Drayton:** A few third-hand tatty chairs; toilets of the old-fashioned kind that would have been there as part of the building—there was no carefully purchased furniture. Wrecking the place? There was nothing to wreck! The toilets were working all the times I was there, though I remember one complaint that a pool ball had been stolen.

The events room can be seen in photos with its whitewashed brick, wooden warehouse doors, tube lights on a board ceiling—it would take a bulldozer plus extraordinary ingenuity to reenact Rome's sacking by the Visigoths upon such a bare industrial space.

In one photo, a note pinned to the wall contains fair irritation muddied by the usual contempt: "please stop covering the wall with your pathetic infantile graffiti! I took the trouble to paint the wall afresh because I (and many others) thought this place was beginning to look like a dosshouse. Predictably, most of the people doing the graffiti were 'anarchist punks' (yes, the sarcasm's meant to be obvious), you may treat where you live as a cesspit but please have some consideration for others!" You'd imagine, if all the fixtures and fittings had been torn out, it might have ranked as a priority worth mentioning over and above the graffiti.

Anarchist sources declare a ramping up of police attention in response to open drug dealing, omnipresent graffiti throughout the neighbourhood, and a rise in general aggro. Michael Clarke is

ANARCHIST CLUBS

The opening of a new Anarchist club [the Autonomy Centre at Wapping in London] is more than an occasion for self-congrat- ulation - though it certainly isn't every day that it happens. There has in fact not been one in this country since we had to close down the old centre at Haverstock Hill (apart from the Centro Iberico squat in Notting Hill). It is a time for appraisal of the purpose and aim of an Anarchist club, and its role in the past and for the future. Whether or not these aims are achieved by the present Autonomy Centre(or the projected Birmingham one) the estab- lishment of a social centre must needs be a key factor in achieving a libertarian movement.

In the early days of the worker's movement, it was a revelation how all branches of what could have been the nuclei of a future society sprang up. Producers' and consumers' co-operatives, community efforts such as bakeries, trade unions, lib- raries, cultural centres. In all of them - except in the creation of a political aide - reformers, radicals, socialists, Marxists, Anarchists, Republicans advocates of women's suffrage, co-operated. It was only when political socialism took prec- edence over everything else and divided the movement that everything but that fell apart or altered course. The trade unions fossilised, the co-op degenerated into a chain store with a democratic constitution, the other collectives for the most part vanished, the workers

clubs became drinking clubs, indistinguishable from any other. With the rise of the Communist Party bitter divisions were set in between sections of the socialist movement while the rise of State Socialism generally brought about the decay of the whole workers' network. The middle class took over the role of socialist leaders and event- ually the Labour Party slid into the present era of backroom pol- itics.

Yet that is not to condemn what it all was in its day, it is merely to mourn its passing. The newer left has over the past few years built up a network of soc- ial activity and particular int- erest: whether this is a new move ment or the shepherding of those who still believe in social change into a special ghetto is a matter for debate. The Anarch- ist nucleus needs to look outwards and certainly for its militants to break away from - and its passive supporters to break out of - the limited and limiting ambiance built up by the package deal left with its prescribed causes and built-in prejudices and tot al isolation from the community the more it describes itself as community politics.

In the thirties there was a theory put forward (which then seemed fantastic) that the battle for the future was between tot- alitarianism on the one hand - with centralism and direction part of the inevitable economic life of any country - and anarchism fighting a losing rear- guard action on the other. But, it was said hopefully, if we could not avoid totalitarianism (and economically we have it as

much in the democratic capit- alist countries as in the state socialist ones) we could at least settle for anarchism in our leisure time, i.e. the state had our working lives but could leave us the rest of our time. We did not need to be regimented from cradle to grave in our lives outside the workplace, and maybe here, it was said, the anarchists had their opportuniy. A neo-an- archism has made this its credo and "dropping out" by any rate for a given period (youth or weekends) became a cult. This overlooks the fact that total- itarianism in crisis always has need to assert itself over private living, but our own views on that are well known. It is important all the same that libertarian influence has been spread by music or through breakaway forms of social living, which gives us a new dimension to the anarchist nucleus.

The role of a club should be to provide a platform for all these diverse social elements - not nec essarily at the same time - and to integrate anarchistic activit- ies with the rest of the comm- unity, without do-gooding domin- ance via rate or state grants, funding itself and acting as a springboard from which other clubs can grow.

Ultimately, such clubs can grow into or foster labour halls. The labour halls of the Labour/TU movement have just decayed into fusty committee rooms. Ideally, a labour hall is the nucleus of a labour movement (which does not have to be state socialist) where people come to exchange jobs nad to get them, to organise their activities at work and make it possible to go from one industry to another; where collectives and co-operative ventures can be formed out of a pool of diver-

sified labour just as can strike committees or support units. This means a whole new libertar- ian labour movement. Is it im- possible to achieve? Given the will and determination of only a few people - and such a move- ment is self-powering - it could be achieved in a matter of months.

Anarchist clubs past and future (*Black Flag* 6, no. 9, November 1981)

Autonomy Centre benefit gig, Sunday 6 December (Courtesy of Mick Slaughter)

less sure: "It's funny *Freedom* mentioned 'drug dealing'—no one had any money! The extent of it would have been a couple of kids with a bag of blues (speed), three for a quid if that! The graffiti consisted of A signs and arrows on the pavements and walls that acted as directions because it was hard to find." Drayton concurs: "There was graffiti inside the centre, yes, but that was true of all the anarchist centres I visited in Europe. As for 'graffiti for blocks around,' it was bitter winter when we were there, snowy and dark and dangerous. No one would roam around Wapping, it's a blatant lie." The weather conditions were so bad that they were described by *Freedom* as a key reason for the Big A Sale's low attendance.

Grant Brand observed police attention, but it was focused more on the anarchists than the punks: "I'm pretty sure we had at least one undercover cop there. He was very interested in asking who the people were who were running the place, and he tried to dress to blend in with the crowd but he didn't look right." Pressure and malevolent attention also emerged from pub and venue owners who took a dim view of the anarchists stealing their potential audience.

> **Bob Short (Blood and Roses):** Wapping (and Centro Iberico) really broke the back of the Lyceum punk gigs. It was more because the Lyceum had been pushing the yobbier side of punk and most people didn't want to get beaten up at gigs—but the promoters held a grudge, they never forgave us. They didn't want anything to do with us before that but when we did get bigger they still kept the doors locked.

> **Michael Clarke:** The venues that complained were the likes of John Curd, a big-time West End promoter, who put on the big gigs at the likes of the Electric Ballroom, Lyceum and Roundhouse. He was worried people would prefer small, self-organised, DIY events with £1 entry, to his £2.50 a head extravaganzas with expensive bars and bow-tied bouncers, thugs, acting as 'security.'

Rudimentary Peni play Wapping
(Courtesy of Paul May)

Autonomy Centre gig,
Sunday 27 December
(Courtesy of Mick Slaughter)

The simultaneous dependence and disrespect the organisers held for the punks was omnipresent. Steve Ignorant visited twice: "I didn't feel welcome, it was very standoffish.... If you hadn't read up on anarchism, they weren't interested in you. Talking to those people, they'd be continually quoting from Malatesta or Bakunin—books I'd never read and found boring. 'Have you read about the Polish miners' strike in 1942?' 'No, I didn't even know it existed, mate!' I thought the idea of anarchism was respect for yourself and for others, or what Flux of Pink Indians said: 'strive to survive causing the least suffering possible.'"

Michael Clarke has written of shelving containing "a library of turgid anarchist tomes":

> When I flicked through one lofty polemic and pointed out that the—World War I–era, Russian, and very dead—author had been a noted antisemite, a bearded anarchist calmly took the book from my hand, replaced it on the shelf, and walked away with a kind of contemptuous flourish worthy of a disgruntled feline. I wasn't an expert on anarchism but, believe it or not, a lot of those books were in my school library and I read some of them, plus my dad had a fascination with George Orwell so I knew about the Spanish Civil War and CNT. We were teenagers but we were also a bit more multifaceted than the stereotype the old beardies painted us all as.[9]

While an unsuccessful anarchist centre, Wapping proved to be a hit as a gig venue with the Scum Collective and Kill Your Pet Puppy Collective attracting a significant array of groups. Even with plenty of people getting in for far less than the £1 entry—if anything at all—one estimate claims the gigs raised nearly £700, averaging about £35–40 every Sunday. Even if that estimate is high, the gigs still represented nearly the only revenue as well as a fair sum.

Instead, the Autonomy Centre tumbled over the precipice after a final gig on 21 February 1982. The landlord, potentially tipped off by the venue's enemies, paid a visit which led to their discovery of, or confirmed, the illicit performances taking place.

ANTHRAX / TRIMINAL DISASTER / FACTION / ??????????? / plus film .

AUTONOMY CENTRE, No: ONE WHAREHOUSE, METROPOLITAN WHARF, WAPPING WALL, E.I.

(APPROX: 4 MINUTES FROM WAPPING TUBE ON METROPOLITAN LINE(EAST LONDON SECTION).

SUNDAY 17th JANUARY 1982.

.TOLD TO ADMIRE ALL LEADERS GREAT & TALL—BUT NEVER TOLD IT WAS THOSE BASTARDS WHO MADE THE PEOPLE CRAWL.

C⊖NFLICT

.TOLD OF GODS GALORE AND HEROES MORE—BUT NEVER OF THOSE WHO WERE BEATEN TO THE FLOOR.

Autonomy Centre gig, Sunday 17 January 1982 (Courtesy of Mick Slaughter)

AUTONOMY CLUB

The Wapping Centre has closed due to lack of support, alas! Most of the furniture and interested people will be now found at the Centro Iberico. A series of 'gigs' (ie musical performances) put on by various bands is planned to occur every Sunday afternnon.

A lack of interest & cash (*Black Flag* VI, no. 11, May 1982)

The beautiful Mr. Tony Drayton: Windy Miller and The Windmills, Sunday 10 January 1982 (Courtesy of Tony Drayton)

Gigs were halted. With rent due on 22 March, the centre mostly emptied of activity, closure was now inevitable.

Little Annie: I went there a couple of times then it all fell apart. There was this sense of 'be yourself ... so long as you're me.' It was kind of exhausting. I'd never read a book on anarchy in my life, I was too busy trying to be one! I thought anarchy was meant to be your own anarchy, not something you needed a degree in. Don't get me wrong, there were a lot of wonderful people doing amazing things, but there were also these people busy telling you, "You shouldn't be doing that; you should be doing this, and you should be doing it this way."

Grant Brand: My experience led me to two conclusions. First, that it was possible for a small group of human beings to work together without the kind of formal power structure associated with an office or factory environment. Such a way of working was less efficient than a formal power structure but was adequate to run a place like the Autonomy Centre. The second conclusion was that, although the formal power structure was absent, there nonetheless existed an informal power structure in which certain people—by virtue of their personalities, gender, physical appearance, etc.—adopted a more dominant role.

Kay Byatt: I wasn't aware of what was going on behind the scenes except for some unrest toward the end. I overheard someone saying, "Well, someone's made money out of this! We're getting ripped off!' Little rumblings like that.

Steve Ignorant: I heard they'd spent all of the money on plastic chairs.

Penny Rimbaud: It wasn't a surprise to us that it didn't work. It was a classic example of anarchism stretched into some form of social order, which inevitably means social conformity and therefore doesn't work because someone is suppressing elements of their own vision.

The Autonomy Centre finally disappeared from *Freedom*'s contact pages in late March: presumably, someone kept the walk-in sessions going until the very end.[10] In the *Shock Slogans* booklet accompanying 1982's *Christ: The Album*, Crass gave a sour epitaph: "Apart from some very good gigs, very little happened. The general feeling is that we were ripped off and that a lot of the money that we, Poison Girls, and many others put into the centre was wasted."

BEGINNINGS AND ENDINGS

By March the music had moved on. Perhaps someone recalled the negotiations back in early 1981 or one of the groups who had played there made the connection. Either way, barely a fortnight after the Sunday swan song in Wapping, the Kill Your Pet Puppy Collective and other supporters were ensconced in a room at Harrow Road beating out a rhythm and chanting "We shall live again!"[1] In May, *Black Flag* belatedly confirmed: "The Wapping Centre has closed due to lack of support, alas! Most of the furniture and interested people will now be found at the Centro Iberico."

As a counterpoint to the negative views of Wapping, for many of the punk contingent, far from a failure, the experience of having a space of their own, was immensely liberating and gave them a sense of empowerment they were able to carry forward into their tumbledown new home.

> **Ruth Doll:** Wapping may have been chaotic and not run as it should have been, but we absolutely loved it! It was like an anarchic youth club and the making of so many of us teens. Centro Iberico was a bit more mature and came with its own history, also other people got involved whereas Wapping was pretty insular. It carried on the good work Wapping started for so many of us and cemented lifelong links so, although they were both only around for that short time, I'm really grateful for them.

Amid this tangled period, García made his final journey: returning to the UK to receive treatment for tuberculosis, he

MIGUEL GARCIA

WE are sad to have to report the death of our friend and comrade, Miguel Garcia, in hospital on Friday 4th December. Everybody who knew Miguel will report on his warmth and life. We shall miss him. Miguel's funeral took place last Thursday, 10th December, attended by about 40 people, from many countries. The following tribute is provided by Albert Meltzer, Miguel's close friend since he came to live in exile in London.

WHEN the military rose in Spain in July 1936, all Barcelona rushed to its defence. Most workers had rushed to CNT unions halls and from there, generally with no more than work and domestic tools — axes, hatchets, knives — surrounded the military government building.

A 28 year old veteran of many struggles since boyhood, Miguel Garcia, gathered up his friends in the plaza Real and they rushed in the *other* direction, up the Ramblas into wealthy Barcelona, storming the gunshops. They collected a formidable round of weapons from a prepared list of sports shops and *then* went to Columbus Square. (A tense moment when they passed an armed Civil Guard squad: whether to go forward or backwards was inviting to be shot in the back. Defiantly they passed, shouting the slogans of the CNT. The Guard saluted. It was loyal to the Popular Front — not to the point of marching to the square to fight the Fascist rebels; but to the point of passively obeying whatever government was.)

It was one of many such incidents in the life of Miguel Garcia who died in London on 4th December. He had spent his youth both in Spain and France and, in the tradition of his family, devoted to building the anarcho-syndicalist unions. He spent the civil war first in the Saragossa campaign, later entirely on the Madrid front. When Franco won he went into a concentration camp which tried to 'rehabilitate' anti-fascists by forced drills. It failed! There he contacted others who intended to fight on and the Resistance that lasted from 1939 to 1949 was initiated.

Others — like Massana, who died earlier in the year — contributed greatly to the tremendous anarchist campaign in the mountains and cities; many made similar sacrifices — he finally was sentenced to death, commuted to 30 years imprisonment (of which he served 20 years).

But what gives Miguel his unique place in libertarian history is not so much the fact of his years of struggling for the Anarchist principle in Spain, but the

fact that after coming out of 20 years solid jail he again came to the front from another new direction, this time on the international field.

He was an inspiration for all the revolutionary Anarchist groups, the Angry Brigade, the First of May Solidarity groupings, the MIL ... as well as others in Spain, Germany and England. He appreciated that the situation in Spain, after years of Francoist repression in which all publicity was given to the Communist Party and the libertarian movement was both suppressed and ignored, meant world attention had to be brought to the Spanish situation and in particular to practical co-operation that would lead to an international different from the various paper internationals.

I was closely associated with him during those years. We organised the international Anarchist Black Cross together, and Miguel went to speak throughout England, Scotland and Wales; in France, Germany, Belgium, Italy, even in East Berlin (we did that by a trick). In all those meetings, fighting against apathy sometimes, with interfering police and harassing Customs officers at other times, he never gave up: he endeared himself to many people throughout the world who admired him for his tenacity and loved him.

When Miguel's book *Franco's Prisoner* came out, another book also appeared, by a Spanish socialist mayor who spent 30 years *In Hiding* — the title of his book. He regarded the anarchists as 'fools' and had spent the three years of repression hiding in a cupboard. Miguel addressed himself to the 'fools' who were activists all over Europe, and refused to admit that State repression was the last word.

ALBERT MELTZER

postscript Because of the many tributes being received about Miguel from all over the world, Black Flag is preparing a special memorial pamphlet outlining his life, work and the last tributes of comrades. Photographs and comment are welcome.

THE prestigious *Sunday Times*, commenting on Tariq Ali's application to join the Labour Party, refers to his membership of the 'revolutionary' Socialist Workers Party. That must please the International Marxist Group, which he has dominated for years. Makes you wonder how many other simple, basic, widely known, easily checkable newspaper 'facts' can be trusted.

AN 865 year jail sentence for embezzlement, in Thailand, has been cut to 576 years, on the grounds that the prisoner's testimony was 'useful'.

Announcement of Miguel García's death (*Freedom* 42, no. 25, 19 December 1981)

died on Friday 4 December 1981. It was decided he would be buried in London with contributions sent to the Direct Action Movement, *Black Flag*, and the Spanish contingent at Centro Iberico. The money raised paid for a funeral at Islington Crematorium on Thursday 10 December, with a circle of forty friends from across Europe paying their respects to a warrior for their cause. García was hailed for helping bring aid to numerous prisoners and comrades across the continent; for helping to rebuild the unions in Spain; for his tirelessness in putting principle into action. The donations gathered were so generous that they paid for the 'Miguel García Memorial Committee' to honour him with a thirty-seven-page booklet, to sit alongside the substantial tributes in the press. Word even reached the anarchy centre's orphans with The Apostles' recording a demo entitled 'For Miguel García.'[2]

Meanwhile, new life bloomed for the newly christened 'Alternative Centre.' An arrangement commenced whereby the Spanish continued their occupancy of the top floor and staged art exhibitions on the second while permitting the punks to share the hall on the first floor.

> **Little Annie:** Even then it was like a time-lapse photo, I remember going there and there were these old Spanish gentlemen sitting drinking together.

> **Kay Byatt:** The squatters would always be there watching, you'd get chatting or you'd wander into their rooms to chat with them. There were Spanish people there, but also people from other countries, it was more international than the Autonomy Centre, more eclectic, but it still had that community vibe.

> **Grant Brand:** In the winter of 1981, I had seen The Mob at the Centro, that was the first time I went there. Prior to that, I had heard it mentioned by Zounds in an interview. It had older Spanish people there which made it feel a bit more

Back in the days when Spanish labour was battling against the ruling class in almost daily strikes (while the rest of Europe the workers were fighting each other in a vain sacrifice to imperialism), in the "anarchist districts" of Barcelona even the newsboys (eight to eleven years old) came out to demand more pay for peddling the daily papers, (pro-German if monarchist, pro-Allied if republican). The proprietors sank their differences on a fight against these fearsome enemies and called out the Guardia Civil. In a cavalry attack upon the newsboys, one armed Guardia Civil feel victim to the stoning – he fell heavily, bleeding from the eye.

The boy – from a home in which father, mother, sisters, brothers were supporters of the CNT (and whose father was one of those who acted as bodyguard to Salvador Segui – the fighting secretary of the unions known affectionately as "Sugarbaby" because his looks belied his toughness) – was assured of support. But Barcelona was not safe for him and he escaped to France.

Thus Miguel Garcia at an early age began his involvement in the international anarchist movement. He came to speak French as well as Spanish. He fought hard in both countries for the libertarian ideal. When the Civil War broke out he drove trucks across the border bringing arms to Spain until stopped. In the Plaza Real, he and his friends and acquaintances gathered together when the fighting broke out. They rushed around Barcelona seizing arms from the gunshops. Had they not done so, the Republic would have starved them of arms to fight the traitor soldiers.

He went to the Saragossa front first, then to the Madrid front where he spend the rest of the Civil war.

When the war ended he fought on against Franco, and was finally sent to a concentration camp where he spent 2½ years for "re-education". But, as he said, he was a "bad pupil". There he met Facerias and the Sabater brothers, and determined, with them, to set up the organisation again once released. They did so. On release they joined the Spanish Resistance (1939-49) of which so little is known.

There were many aspects to it: the smuggling of arms and people over the frontier and down the mountains from or to Barcelona. The re-organisation of the unions of the CNT. The sabotage against Franco and especially against the Axis war effort. One by one the heros of the Resistance – bandits after 1939 according to Franco, but only after 1945 according to the Allies! – fell to ambushes. Only a few survived. Massana, who died recently, "last of the mountain guerrillas". Miguel Garcia, who died in London on the morning of December 4th this year: urban fighter in France, organiser of illegal printing presses in Barcelona, part of the chain for escapees in Catalonia.

Like many others Miguel was caught and went to prison for 20 years (after a death sentence had been commuted) owing to international pressure). He writes of this graphically in his book "Franco's Prisoner". His comrade-in-arms died, but he managed to survive. And after coming out he entered into a new struggle. Speaking fluent Italian, impeccable French and not quite so good English, he decided to go abroad and denounce the Franco regime; organise fresh resistance and work towards the future. Without a penny, with nothing to back him but sheer guts, he came and joined us in the Black Cross in London.

He spoke all over England and Scotland, but also in West Germany – East Berlin too by a ruse – France, Belgium, Italy. . . I remember so well driving him from town to town and the whoops of our delighted singing after we had passed a forbidden frontier (the Franco police never queried an English car!)

When Miguel's book came out it was widely reviewed, usually compared with another book "In Hiding" about a Socialist major, also an opponent of Franco, who regarded the anarchists as "fools". In the preface to the German version of "Franco's Prisoner" Miguel commented typically that the mayor had spent thirty years hiding in a cupboard just as — for that matter — had German socialism. His book was for the 'fools', in Germany and elsewhere, who resisted. His creed was: In front of tyranny, no compromise, no quarter.

This paper owes a great debt to Miguel Garcia for his advice, experience (and grumbling, sometimes, too). What the international revolutionary movement owes him no one will ever fully know. His contacts in Spain made it possible for us to help a large number of libertarian prisoners; but his contacts were not only in Spain. All over Europe there are people he helped one way or another (a **real internationalist, he was just as** much concerned in helping people to squat in London as re-building the union movement in Catalonia). At the time of his death he was trying to see if he could visit the States on a lecture tour "and after that, I'll come to Africa with you."

Miguel died of TB after a hard life but one well worth while. He has been a great inspiration to us all.

ALBERT MELTZER

MIGUEL GARCIA

A PERSONAL APPRECIATION

I first met Miguel in 1973. He was then 67 but could easily have been mistaken for a man in his late 40's. Squarely-built, a shock of thick black hair brushed straight back from his forehead, bespectacled, and dressed casually in check work shirt and corduroy trousers, he was anything but the popular image of a Spanish Anarchist. I had expected him to be an old man, bowed down by his twenty years in Franco's prisons. Not a bit of it. Instead, he seemed to have been actually preserved by his years inside; held in suspended animation whilst he stored up energy and ideas for action. He had not witnessed the years of defeat and internal squabbling which had taken the life out of the Spanish Libertarian Movement in exile. He had gone into prison fighting, and that was the way he had come out.

Miguel's comrades in arms, who had fought in the civil war had gone on fighting in the 'peace' — refusing the recognise defeat — no longer functioned in any organised way by the time he was released in 1969. Most were dead, still in prison, or in exile. But a new generation had sprung up whilst Miguel was inside to carry on the work of the libertarian Resistance. As soon as he was released, Miguel plunged straight back into the struggle again., as International Secretary of the newly-reformed Anarchist Black Cross. Bringing practical aid to libertarian prisoners all over the world, and making solidarity an effective springboard to militant action, the aim of the Black Cross was to build a revolutionary anarchist International; not on paper, but out of deeds. This was instrumental in re-structuring the Resistance and (through the FOI) keeping alive the libertarian traditions in the Spanish workers' movement that led to the re-emergence of the CNT. As a result of helping the anarchist fighters in Spain such activity activated anarchist movement in many other parts of the world, including Britain, France, Belgium, and West Germany. Miguel's part in all this was immeasureable.

My introduction to the revolutionary anarchist movement was through the campaign of solidarity with the resistance groups of the MIL, and in particular the attempts to save one of their members, Salvador Puig-Antich, from the garrot. Puig-Antich was put to death with this mediaeval instrument at 4am, on 2nd March 1974. Miguel had met the young Catalan anarchist and liked him. But typically his concern was for the living, for continuing the struggle.

like a social club or community centre. The Autonomy Centre was a better place to play a gig, it was more intimate and the audience felt more sympathetic because it was a smaller bunch of people we knew, rather than a larger group of punks who were uncomfortable with our rather 'nonpunk mainstream' image. They were appreciative, but you always felt you might get something chucked at you at any minute!

Phil Barker: What struck me was the size of the place! People living upstairs, big space used for gigs, walls all painted—it was very different to the austere concrete of Wapping.

Tony Drayton: Come up the stairs and there's a small landing. The room with the stage is straight ahead while to the left was this side room which had all this old-fashioned and wrecked furniture and huge windows so it was full of light. This was the room where we sold the literature left behind by the anarchists at Wapping when we tidied it up, and where Brett sold food. We took loads of anarchist magazines up to the Alternative Centre and started selling them for a penny each or giving them away, which really annoyed the people from *Class War* and *Freedom*: "Why are you giving our stuff away?" And we'd tell them, "You left it! It was all going to be chucked in the bin." This was all upstairs and it was really quite chilly, March in the old school was quite cold.

The site veritably buzzed with life for the next eight months with confirmed gigs on all but three of the twenty-five weekends from early March to mid-August. Kill Your Pet Puppy put out an appeal in their *Alternative Centre Sunday Supplement* for equipment including chemical toilets, tape recorders, a plugboard, paint and brushes, food/tea/coffee, plus smaller things like bin bags and drum sticks.

Andy Martin: My initial impressions were of a partly derelict space in need of soap, disinfectant and bin-liners. However, where the Spanish anarchists lived on the third floor, it was spotlessly clean and tidy. When we first started working there—and by working I really do mean work: cleaning the place up, throwing out the rubbish, painting and decorating, repairing the electric circuitry, installing the plumbing—some of it had already been started by members of Assassins of Hope and Hagar the Womb. The credit for making Centro Iberico available as a concert space goes to those two groups of people.

The venue was significantly less isolated than Wapping. At 389 Harrow Road, Aswad and others recorded at Addis Ababa Studios, while the Windsor Castle pub at No. 309 had hosted U2, The Jam, and Madness. Acklam Hall community centre under the Westway dual carriageway was a key venue before going on hiatus from 1981 to 1985. The Meanwhile Gardens hosted gigs across the canal in Westbourne Park. Just five minutes away at 22 Great Western Road, the Zig Zag Club opened in April 1982 and staged shows until closing on 8 August.[3]

Friday 5 March: Zounds, The Mob, Null and Void and Youth in Asia. Except for Youth in Asia, the bands had played an August 1981 date at Centro Iberico then a December gig together in Wapping. Grant Brand of Rudimentary Peni remembers the show being sparsely attended, presumably because word was still getting round about the new home.

Mark Hedge (Null and Void): I remember a lot of black and red clothing, flags, banners, a lot of spiky hair, plenty of dogs about, plenty of trips to the off-license. A real energy about the place. Just being there or playing there felt like a political statement. This was a meeting of tribes. Tribes of misfits. Tribes of people failed by the education system, failed by the state, tired of the system of government—a lot of like-minded people. We shared a passionate hatred

THE FUNERAL OF MIGUEL GARCIA

This photo was taken in North London when the body of our comrade Miguel Garcia (see last issue) was taken to the Islington Crematorium. An impressive number of comrades from a dozen countries paid their last respects. The funeral was paid for by contributions from Direct Action Movement, Black Flag, Centro Iberico and members and comrades from overseas, leaving a healthy balance with which we are starting a Miguel Garcia Publications Fund. The first will be *Miguel Garcia's Story* containing some autobiographical chapters (omitted from *Franco's Prisoner)* and tributes with biographical notes. Anyone wanted to be associated with the tributes should write to the Flag for the leaflet.

The Funeral of Miguel García (*Black Flag* VI, no. 11, May 1982)

I would like to thank all comrades who contributed so generously to Miguel Garcia's funeral. We not only have paid all funeral expenses but have £100 in hand, with more coming in, from people who desired to be associated with this tribute.

The balance, with anything else that has still to come in, will be used to produce a memorial pamphlet to which a number of his friends have contributed.

A Meltzer

Paying respects to Miguel García
(*Freedom* 43, no. 2, 6 February 1982)

of the Conservative Party and Margaret Thatcher and were ready for the system to collapse, willing it with our thoughts and deeds. It never felt like 'just another gig,' it was always an event.

The strong initial lineup of bands was helped because the landlord stopped shows in Wapping after many bands had already confirmed for March and April. Of the sixteen bands noted as 'coming soon!' and 'forthcoming attractions!' ten simply switched over to the Alternative Centre.

Andy Martin (The Apostles): We would organise one gig, then the next weekend the Pet Puppy lot would organise a gig—nothing during the week, or at least I'm not aware of any because I was a youth worker at the time so worked all week. We booked performance artists and whatnot too. I'd like to shout out Peter North, who was a solo performance artist; also 12Cubic Feet, Amsterdammed from Holland; a band with a superb flute player called The Replaceable Heads—they counterbalanced the punk-rockery.

Word of mouth between those in the know, fly-posting the local area and tube stations, an old blackboard at the school repurposed for gig notices, six mentions in *Sounds* gig listings over the summer ... It was enough to build fair audiences.

Bob Short: We never advertised, I don't think we knew how. Mostly, if you were asked to play, you played because there was nothing else happening, you were either in your squat or hanging out at someone else's. If you were lucky, you still had enough dole left to buy a bottle of cider. Everything was done by word of mouth.

Hugh Vivian (Omega Tribe): Other people's bands would get you in: "Do you wanna play this place?" It was all very DIY. If we had a gig, there were a few bands we would then try and support by asking, "Can this band play too?"

Miguel García's Story by the Miguel García Memorial Committee
(Cienfuegos Press, 1982)

Kay Byatt: You would chat to people at gigs or write them letters. I relied on a telephone box outside where I was living. People would ring me and whoever was passing by would answer the phone and then knock on my window so I could come out and take the call.

Steve Pegrum (The Sinyx): There was a great letter-writing network that emanated from the fanzine scene. Also the tape-trading network was very important because we'd always have our addresses on them so, again, we might get offered gigs from there.

Alternative Centre opening, March 1982 (Courtesy of Tony Drayton)

The Mob, Zounds, Null and Void, Youth in Asia, Friday 5 March 1982

Lou and Tim in the playground (Courtesy of Mick Lugworms)

Louise Challice arriving (Courtesy of Mick Lugworms)

Trevor with Ivan Oxo at the school door (Courtesy of Mick Lugworms)

**Val Puppy making
use of the old school
furniture (Courtesy of
Kill Your Pet Puppy)**

**Val Puppy flanked by Green Hair and W (William Ogden) by the Downstairs Stage
(Courtesy of Val Puppy)**

LET'S START A WAR ...

A well-remembered incident took place at Rudimentary Peni's gig with Part One on Sunday 14 March 1982. Grant Brand was told that Annie Anxiety (aka Little Annie), who was working with Crass, was in the audience with oi 'superstar' Wattie Buchan whose band, The Exploited, had been on *Top of the Pops* the previous year.

Little Annie: I went there with Wattie. I'd met him a few days before at the 100 Club and he was really nice! I knew there was a gig happening so I took him over to Centro Iberico which was maybe a dumb move on my part but I was trying to expose him to something else—and they threw something all over his head. Some gloop or something. It was fucked up: "Anarchy and peace.... And we're going to throw something over somebody's head!"

Andy Martin: There's this Scottish punk cornered with various punky types all hurling abuse or yelling questions like an inquisition—I was horrified. I told them they were bullying him and they told me I didn't realise this was Wattie Buchan of The Exploited—what justification did that give them to intimidate the fella? One of the Pet Puppy crew said, "Don't you realise this fellow put out a track called 'Fuck the Mods'?" In those days I dressed like a mod: two-tone suit, porkpie hat, Ben Sherman shirt ... I just wasn't a fan of the music. "So? Are you saying he's not allowed? I don't like punks! Am I not allowed to release a song attacking punks?" I like to think my defence of him meant maybe he decided not all mods were bastards.

Kay Byatt: Poor old Wattie! I remember someone saying, "You'll never guess who just turned up! What the fuck's he doing here?" All these anarcho-punks surrounded him and Annie was looking quite frazzled by all this going on. They were trying to get a reaction and he handled it very well, he was calm and eloquent. This kind of us-and-them thinking had started to appear and some bands were looked at differently. I thought they were putting themselves to shame—he was entitled to be there! Someone shouted, "Why are you here?" and Wattie said, "Because I want to be!" Then Annie, "I asked him to be here. What's the problem?" In the end, he hung about in the kitchen, watched some bands, then they probably did head off.

Passionate arguments were playing out in the music press regarding the virtues of oi with Gary Bushell of *Sounds* proving a lightning rod for both celebration and criticism from all sides, including being attacked by British Movement members at an Angelic Upstarts gig at the 100 Club in December 1981.[1] In the aftermath of Rock Against Racism and the Anti-Nazi League freezing out attempts by the National Front and British Movement to legitimise racism and anti-immigrant sentiment in the music scene, some felt oi was sympathetic to fascism, which is unfair. Others were nervous of the skinhead look, or disdained the 'cartoonish' coloured mohawks. Still others disliked its resurrection of punk's more yobbish sentiments that many had hoped had been left behind with Sid Vicious and can best be summed up in *VIZ* comic's mock advertising poster: "A Pint And A Fight—A Great British Night."

Hugh Vivian: You didn't know how people's politics might align so anarcho-punk bands wouldn't necessarily play with bands like GBH or The Exploited. You could

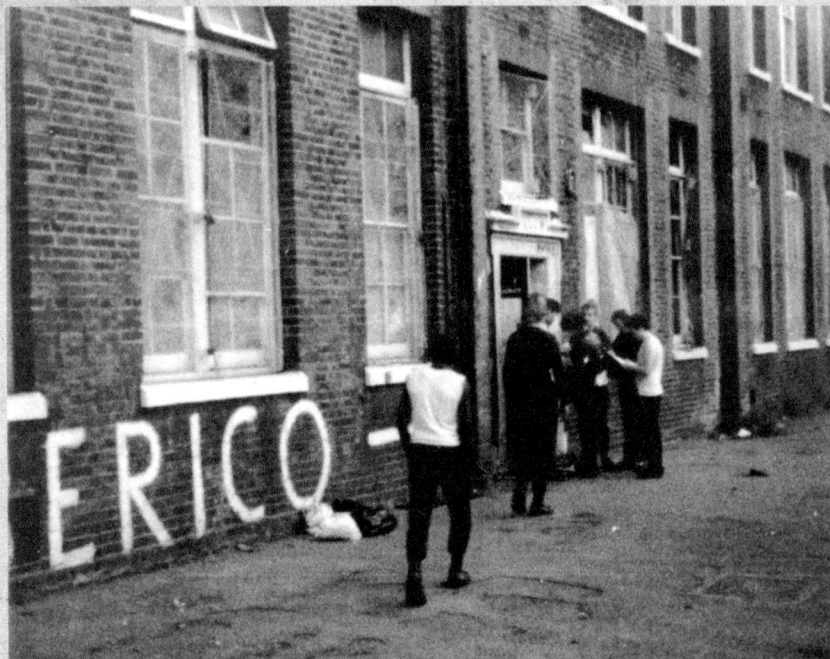

Manning the front door at Centro Iberico (Courtesy of Michael Baxter)

legitimately do a crude class division: it was fair to say a lot of anarcho-punk originated with people who were less working class, more aligned with free thinking and political traditions like anarchism or had a bit of involvement in the hippy or free festival movements. Gary Bushell was advocating for what he claimed was working-class punk. Oi didn't really have a politics, it was more "We're the kids, this is what we do, if you don't like it, fuck off!"

Tony Drayton: The oi movement was more about fighting and football, so the antithesis of what we were doing, our anarchism and pacifism stuff. There was a feeling of 'the enemy,' of punk being split into two camps. Annie bought Wattie over and he was fine, I shook his hand, and he said: "It's a great thing you've got going here! Can I play here?" I said, "Probably best not, but you could organise it if you like."

ALTERNATIVE

We're working working

in late 79/early 80,

After the Persons Unknown

Anarchist Conspiracy Trial, Iris Mills and Ronan Bennett

decided to set up an Anarchist Centre in London.

the Poison Girls and Crass became interested

and agreed to donate the proceeds of a single to the centre.

With so many of today's youngsters lining up in the dole queue it's good news when you meet a few who have managed to make it alone. They're their own bosses and success has meant working all hours, but when you're doing what you want in life, who cares?

"It's no longer the old posey decadence. It's the real thing. People are not just talking about it anymore they are actually living it."

— very happy teenagers indeed

ANARCHY IN WAPPING

in 1981, premises were found in a warehouse in Wapping

.The first Autonomy Centre was born. by November it was discovered that

there wasn't enough money coming in to pay the rent.(£50 a week the Scum

Collective arranged a benefit gig.Enough money was made to pay

that weeks rent and it was decided to have meetings and gigs every Sunday.

THE NEW CHURCH

Before the Wapping Centre,the meeting place for many of those who were

later to form the Autonomy Centre had been the St.James' church squat in

the Pentonville Rd. Somehow out of the chaos an atmosphere developed.

something was starting to happen again.

Unfortunately,before we fully appreciated the place,it caught fire, did

AT Wapping we found a new church.It was still chaotic,but we

were learning how to handle it-spontaneous organisation!

And it was fun,it was more than just another venue,becuase anyone

could get involved on the door,behind the bar,on stage

helping to clear up at the end —

"I asked myself: 'Why don't I take it over?'

IT WAS COLD AND IT SNOWED

All through the winter more and more people found their way despite the

blizzards,to the Metropolitan Warf.There wasn't much inside,a couple of bare

rooms,soon covered with posters,graffitti and paintings;no heating,a dodgy

kettle,tidal toilets,a tiny stage and a smaller p.a.There were usually

six bands a night,weather permitting.Drink,food,tea,coffee and

literature provided at bargain prices.

NOTHING LASTS...

Then,just as we felt we were managing to achieve something,the landlord

stepped in to stop the noise.It was February.With no entertainments

licence,no fire licence,no drinks licence and no proper lease,it looked

like the end.No gigs,no money,no centre.

A Mersey Docks

Al Puppy (aka Alistair Livingston)'s first Iberico tale (Courtesy of Kill Your Pet Puppy)

had but were for ourselves

Sometimes it is called Movement For Gay Vegetarian Abortionists (Living In Squats, Getting Stoned On The Heretical Sciences), or more simply the Lost Tribe. *Alternative*

NO MORE COMPROMISE
LOVE IS THE LAW

CENTRE

NOT JUST ANOTHER VENUE

IT could be the beginnings of an upheaval as profound as punk — these seeds of dis-satisfaction do have a habit of growing once they have germinated.

"WE SHALL LIVE AGAIN"

We weren't going to let it die. The Sunday gigs had given us the confidence, given the chance it could happen again. Anarchists survive. Within two weeks we had the use of a couple of rooms in a Spanish anarchist squat. The first meeting was beautifully chaotic -no equipment no bands and about 20 people; just like the old days. We improvised, tribal percussion with pieces of wood, cider bottles and lager cans - a chant,"we shall live again...".Slowly we did.

BUILD YOUR OWN @ CENTRE

Again there could be no publicity, due to eviction threats..again we began to break down the barriers between spectators and participants, between audience and organisers. At least now there was a kitchen, a proper stage and a room to talk and read in. It wasn't easy, every week another crisis, another nervous breakdown, no mikes, no drums, no food, no van, no lights - the police are here, someone just got arrested....the toilets blocked. Eventually it all began to work, to prove our point. Anarchy is a promise, not a threat. And people are enjoying it.

ALL FOR £1

On Sunday 2nd May 1982, after one mention in the gig listings, over 500 people turned up to see Rubella Ballet, Conflict, The Apostles, The Assassins of Hope and Amsterdammed. 400 managed to squeeze in. We made £35, but the important thing was that it happened.

HERE WE GO AGAIN

Now we were ready for the next step. Before the 2nd May, approaches had been made by major venues seeking collaboration, the chance to use more publicity to reach a wider audience to claim that we had "won". But if we have the potential to attract 2000(one venue's estimate) why should we start working through the straight business now? Why not try and go a bit further on our own?

We are ready for the next move. Plus whatever anarchic insanity we can

URBAN GUERILLAS IN MAKE UP

We intend to go with the energy that is building up -to the limits of our expectations and beyond. With these events we intend to demonstrate what can be done by anyone -Organise the Imagination! They are just the outward manifestation of a process of anarchic alchemy -its not boring politics or simplistic slogans -its everything your parents warned you against. Out of the ruins of this society we are creating our own lives, a new world in our hearts.

LACK OF KNOWLEDGE.
DEAD SOULS.   BLOOD & ROSES.
TWELVE CUBIC FEET.
APOSTLES.   VERTICAL HOLD.

21ST MARCH   1982
CENTRO IBERICO, HARROW ROAD, W.9.
7·30 P.M.   ONE POUND.

A busy night on stage, Sunday 21 March

This isn't just a gig venue run by an elite clique of people – our last Sunday Supplement ("A Kick Up the Arse!!") produced a good response, unfortunately the week after it was handed out we were out of Wapping and here on Harrow Rd – everything said in 'Kick Up the Arse' still applies here:

"If you dont put energy into the centre well get pissed off and put none in ourselves and then where will you be? The Lyceum? The Clarendon? 100 club? Twice the cost, half the bands, and bouncers = no fun. Thieves, no-one paying, no participation = no Ⓐ Centre.
Its your centre, use it dont abuse it" etc.etc.

When a new, permanent place is found that we can use during the daytime for more than just gigs, then these gigs now should have raised enough to pay for facilities and things that can be used by and for all.

If you have any ideas about what should be there in an Ⓐ Centre then, as before, come along early and discuss it.

Crass have shown an interest in helping out, but they dont want to be used as a money source (the way Iris Mills and crew did in the setting up of the last place) – this place has to be financially independent here, then they will feel more confident that any time/energy/money they put into a new centre wont be wasted or squandered like last time.

Hopefully there will be an Animal Liberation film shown here soon, before the bands come on – if anyone knows of anyway to get similar films to show let someone know, we will also have a slide projector here very soon, so any slides anyone has will be gratefully recieved. Ⓐ Windy

FORTHCOMING GIGS

ALL £1 entry, we open at 4.30pm, first band on at 7pm, finish 10.30pm.

21st March: 12 Cubic Feet/Apostles/ Lack of Knowledge/Replaceable Heads.

28th March: Rubella Ballet (to be confirmed)/ Action Pact/Dead Mans Shadow.

4th April: The Subhumans/Organised Chaos/ Locusts/Hagar the Womb.

11th April: EASTER – no trains? no bands! probably a free, mind boggling, weird and wonderful day.

18th April: Flux (to be confirmed)/Cold War/Screaming Babies.

25th April: The Mob/Bikini Mutants/D-notice?

THE ALTERNATIVE CENTRE IS AT: CENTRO IBERICO 421a Harrow Rd, W9 EVERY SUNDAY (an old school) 5 mins from Westbourne Pk Ⓞ buses 28,31,36b,18

And a bustling March–April at Centro Iberico (Courtesy of Kill Your Pet Puppy)

Youth in Asia, Saturday 17 April (Courtesy of Mick Slaughter)

MIND-BOGGLING, WEIRD, WONDERFUL

For Easter, envisaging limited public transport and family obligations, Kill Your Pet Puppy included a note in a flyer: "EASTER—no
trains? No bands? Probably a free, mind-boggling, weird and
wonderful day." It was indeed: Andy Martin confirms that a poetry
and film evening took place for those individuals who made the
trek across town.

Gig lineups could change at no notice if bands proved unable
to make a date, or because someone turned up just wanting a
chance if a gap in festivities presented itself. As an example, Bob
Short of Blood and Roses remembers a mix-up in which "we were
supposed to play but the other bands didn't seem to know and
we ended up doing a three-song set." The Cult of the Supreme
Being—a scratch group formed by Robert Dellar with members of
bands from around Watford like Mex and The S-Haters—made it
on stage before breaking up in March. Dellar's The Nasty Godless
Pinkoes and Paul Mex's Gambit of Shame had been pencilled in
for Wapping, so it seems they did fulfil their gig obligation but at
the new venue. Peter North, who ran the gloriously idiosyncratic
Rosy Recordings tape label, was part of a line up with obscure
groups Replaceable Heads and The Invisible Band on another
unknown night.

As at Wapping, a core circle once again shouldered the work
required to control the door, ensure the toilets were sanitary,
handle any issues and clear up afterwards—sometimes gritting
their teeth when a certain percentage of audience members
proved less than considerate as Andy Martin describes: "It was
a bone of contention with John (Soares) and I that, after each gig,

121 Bookshop Benefit
Sunday May 2nd
6.30pm
Centro Iberica
42/A Harrow Road
Westbourne Park—tube
Adm £1 Booze, Food, Music
Zounds, Rubella Ballet, Conflict,
Assassins of Hope, Amsterdamned.

121 Anarchist Centre benefit, Sunday 2 May 1982
(*Freedom* 43, no. 7, 17 April 1982)

121 ANARCHIST CENTRE
BENEFIT

with Rubella Ballet, Zounds,
Assassins of Hope,
Conflict & Amsterdamned

at Centro Iberico,
421a Harrow Road, W10
Westbourne Park underground

6.30pm on Sunday 2nd May
£1

121 Anarchist Centre benefit,
Sunday 2 May 1982 (*Black Flag*
VI, no. 11, May 1982)

A strong lineup for the 121, Sunday 2 May

it was the same people—namely members of Hagar the Womb, Kill Your Pet Puppy, and ourselves—sweeping up all the beer tins, fag packets, and whatnot. Few other people bothered to help. At the end of one event, Fox and Vomit from DIRT were seen armed with brooms helping clean up—these two stalwarts behaved brilliantly."

Residual ties with the anarchist movement in London led to a major benefit gig taking place for Brixton's 121 Centre which was under threat of eviction. 121 Railton Road had been squatted since 1973 and by the early 80s contained the 121 Bookshop, the 121 Café, acted as a meeting point for numerous left-wing political groups and elements of the squatting network, housed the Kate Sharpley Library anarchist archive, and hosted the Anarchist Black Cross after 1978.

Advertisements in the anarchist press on top of the punks' methods affected awareness of Centro Iberico, such that the old school hall welcomed an estimated four hundred people with a further hundred listening from outside in the playground. The stage was crowded too with five bands playing: Rubella Ballet, Conflict, The Apostles, Assassins of Hope, and Amsterdammed.

> **Chantal Davey (Assassins of Hope):** It was packed to capacity. The 'Highbury Hit Squad' were there to support us, friends and supporters from the old Autonomy Centre. The name was a bit misleading: a fanzine writer had said we sounded like Arsenal supporters and, unfortunately, had said this to Peat (Protest) who headbutted him to show his displeasure! During our set, the Hit Squad invaded the stage numerous times shouting, "You've got no fucking hoile!"—Welsh for guts/bollocks—at the audience. It was a really good, crowd-pleasing gig and we enjoyed ourselves, though Sid (Truelove) from Rubella Ballet was distressed as it was his drum kit onstage and it was later reported that Assassins of Hope were not to be let near anyone's instruments!

Support from the anarchist community included Stuart Christie and Cienfuegos Press providing prizes for 'the Cienfuegos

Disaster Fund Draw' consisting of a first prize of two Lopi Wool jumpers "handknitted in Orcadian 'Magus' patterns," with Orcadian food hampers for second and third. Kill Your Pet Puppy summed up the success as: "We made £35, but the important thing was that it happened." Not a bad outcome given an audience of skint youths.

DIY ODD ACTS

The residents and their new guests remained on cordial terms with Eduardo Niebla recalling: "The punks just ran their own stuff and would clean up afterwards. I would keep an eye out because people kept breaking the walls in the stairwell so I'd repair them the next day." On Sunday 16 May, the Spanish booked their entertainment into the first-floor assembly hall with Lady June and various people associated with the band Gong staging 'An Odd Acts Event' featuring "a hilarious story by Lol Coxhill.... Some solo poems by Daevid Allen, and Gilli Smyth's performance accompanied by extracts from Harry Williamson's Tarka, as well as Lady June's own performance."[1]

Unfortunately, a lack of coordination meant the Alternative Centre had also booked bands, turning up to find the residents' event already in motion. Tony Drayton: "We all sat in the dark downstairs on the ground floor until this old Spanish guy said, 'If you fix it up, you can do your gigs down here if you like.' After that, we never used the upstairs again except for doing food in the side room." A sensible compromise, the move ignited another bout of industriousness including building a stage from old gas cookers and doors covered in carpet; soundproofing the walls; ensuring the electricity supply was safe to use; and decorating the old gymnasium.

> **Tony Drayton:** To build the stage, we went round the streets trying to find old furniture and we came back with this old cooker someone had found in a skip then we built all kinds of bits around it—that was the base. It was quite

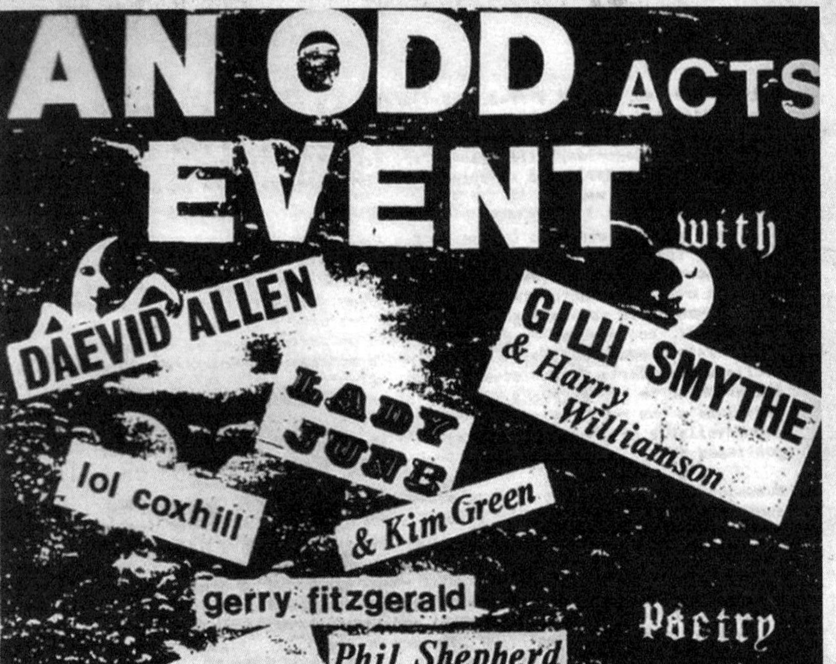

An Odd Acts Event, Sunday 16 May 1982

small, not the whole end of the room or anything. One of the brainwaves was to put it sideways: you came in through the door into a hallway and to the right, there wasn't a door, it was just an archway, a space to differentiate the hallway from the hall itself. Putting the stage sideways, it naturally faced out into the hallway—turning one room into two. People said it wouldn't work because there wasn't enough space between the stage and the end of the room but people just naturally filled the space, they used both rooms. Also, I went and got all this paint and we started to paint it up. I did this big pyramid across a whole wall, like an Illuminati symbol with an eye, then we came in one day and people had used the leftover paint to do graffiti and their own murals. They'd done all this random stuff all over it.

On the ground floor at the back, you were in this corridor and you'd go along it to where we had the fuse box and all the toilets—though, of course, the whole playground was kind of a toilet.... This guy Wolfen, he was a punk, but he worked as an electrician so he knew how to run power from this giant fuse box—almost a room in itself, this terrifying electrical room. He put wires into it and had them running all up the wall, then he moved a ladder all the way along nailing the wires to the roof. Next, he put together this big board with lots of plugs and sockets, like a big extension lead, and put that by the stage so bands could put five or six plugs into it.

After the Alternative Centre's move into the newly refreshed gymnasium, the residents continued to invite guests upstairs. Jordi Valls reconnected with his Spanish friends to book a gig for power electronics innovators Whitehouse on Saturday 1 May, and a return on Saturday 12 June—postponed from Saturday 5 June. Philip Best's Consumer Electronics appeared on 12 June, while the performance art troupe Neo-Naturists appeared on both occasions.

DEATH IS REALITY TODAY DEATH IS REAL

THE CENTRO IBERICO   FRIDAY JUNE 4th   7.30 - 11.00pm.
421A HARROW ROAD, LONDON W.9   DIRT/ANTHRAX
HEIR ATTACK / THE OMEGA TRIBE

THE WHITE LION   THURSDAY JUNE 10th   7.30 - 11.00pm.
PUTNEY (NEAREST TUBE PUTNEY BRIDGE)
DIRT / YOUTH IN ASIA

THE FRONT LINE THEATRE   FRIDAY JUNE 11th   7.30 - 11.00pm
ATLANTIC ROAD, BRIXTON (FROM BRIXTON. TUBE OR OVERGROUND UNDER THE
BRIDGE TURN RIGHT INTO COLD HARBOUR LANE,
THEN RIGHT INTO ATLANTIC ROAD).
DIRT / ANTHRAX / BENJAMIN

THE RED LION
GRAVESEND (NEAREST STATION BRITISH RAIL GRAVESEND)
DIRT / THE OMEGA TRIBE

THE MOONLIGHT CLUB
WEST HAMPSTEAD (NEAREST TUBE WEST HAMPSTEAD)

DIRT   ANTHRAX

ALL GIGS £1.00 each

TY TODAY DEATH IS REALITY DEATH IS REAL

THE CENTRO IBERICO
DIRT / ANTHRAX / THE OMEGA TRIBE /
HEIR ATTACK / Friday 4th June /
THE WHITE LION PUTNEY
DIRT / YOUTH IN ASIA / Thursday 10th June
THE FRONT LINE CLUB
BRIXTON / Friday 11th June
DIRT / ANTHRAX / BENJAMIN
THE RED LION GRAVESEND
DIRT / THE OMEGA TRIBE / Tuesday 15th June
THE MOONLIGHT WEST HAMPSTEAD
DIRT / ANTHRAX / Sunday 20th June
ALL GIGS £1.00 each
START 7.30 — 11.00pm

**DIRT, Anthrax, Heir Attack, and The Omega Tribe,
Friday 4 June 1982 (Courtesy of Mick Slaughter)**

LONDON. Bridge House, Canning Town, (01-476 2889), **Wasted Youth**
LONDON. Centro Iberico, Harrow Road, **Dirt/Anthrax/Hair Attack**
LONDON. Dingwalls, Camden Lock, (01-267 4967), **Firing Squad/Penguin Fury**
LONDON. Dominion Theatre, (01-580 9562), **Rory Gallagher**
LONDON. Dublin Castle, Camden, (01-485 1773), **Tex Axile And The Dodgers**
LONDON. Feltham Football Club, **Dynamite Band**
LONDON. Golden Lion, Fulham, (01-385 3942), **Idle Flowers**
LONDON. Half Moon, Herne Hill, (01-737 4580), **A Bigger Splash/The Pals**
LONDON. Half Moon, Putney, (01-788 2387), **Hank Wangford**
LONDON. Hammersmith Odeon, (01-748 4081), **Camel**
LONDON. Hogs Grunt, Production Village, Cricklewood, (01-450 8969), **Root Jackson/The Tucker Finlayson Band/U-Crane**
LONDON. Hope And Anchor, Upper Street, Islington, (01-359 4510), **Roddy Radiation And The Tearjerkers**
LONDON. Kings Head, Fulham, (01-736 1413), **Little Sister**
LONDON. New Golden Lion, Fulham, (01-385 3942), **Tony McPhee**
LONDON. Old White Horse, Brixton, (01-487 3440), **Seething Wells/Amazulu**
LONDON. 100 Club, Oxford Street, (01-636 0933), **Paz**
LONDON. Rock Garden, Covent Garden, (01-240 3961), **The Inversions**
LONDON. Roebuck, King's Road, (01-352 7611), **Harfoot Bros**
LONDON. Roebuck, Tottenham Court Road, **Design For Living**
LONDON. The Ship, Plumstead Common, **Cerious B/Negative Response**
LONDON. The Venue, Victoria Street, (01-828 9441), **Mood Six/Marble Staircase/The Poetic Slav**
*LONDON. Zig Zag Club, Great Western Road, (01-289 6008), **Rip Rig And Panic**

DIRT, Anthrax, and Heir Attack gig, Friday 4 June (*Sounds*, 5 June 1982)

NDON. Bridge House, Canning Town, (01 426 2889), **Lone Wolf**
NDON. Bull And Gate, Kentish Town, (01 485 5358), **Ricky Cool**
NDON. Centro Iberico, Harrow Road, **White House/Neo-Naturistic** abaret

The cancelled Whitehouse date, Saturday 5 June (*Sounds*, 5 June 1982)

LONDON. Centro Iberico, Harrow Road, Whitehouse/Neo-Naturist Cabaret

Whitehouse gig, Saturday 12 June (*Sounds*, 12 June 1982)

Grayson Perry, who would later become one of Britain's most notorious contemporary artists, describes the May date in his memoir. "We were booked to do a Neo-Naturist performance … at the Spanish Anarchists Association, which was similar to a working men's club, an extremely anachronistic place that had become somehow hip because of punk's associations with anarchy. As it was May, Fiona thought we should do a Communist, May Day–themed cabaret. Cerith, Fiona, Jen, Angela and I all had identical Communist uniforms body painted on to us with khaki paint and we decorated ourselves with big red five-pointed stars," he recalled. "There were around a hundred anarchists in the audience as well as some punks and they all hated it, not one of them clapped, the room was dead quiet."[2]

Later in the year, on Saturday 21 August, Eduardo Niebla himself put together a quintet and made the effort to get it listed in *Sounds*. The decision to play a Saturday meant it wouldn't clash with the following evening's punk gig. While the Spanish put on other shows for which we lack flyers or listings, it's also true that a much-reduced number of core residents remained by 1982 given the building's relatively inhospitable living conditions.

WEEKENDS OF ACTION

The generally harmonious flow of events at Centro Iberico was, of course, subject to occasional disruption, accidental or otherwise. Gary Buckley of DIRT explains: "There were three weekends of planned gigs.[1] We went to the Conflict gig and Conflict didn't show up. Regular/resident anarchy bands played.... The following week we went to see Flux of Pink Indians—lo and behold, they didn't show up. Same resident bands played.... Midweek I got a phone call from a guy called Dan. He informed me the gig had been cancelled but I knew Dan—it wasn't him on the phone! I phoned Dan and he told me the gig was still on.... So we showed up as planned. The Apostles, Assassins of Hope, and Hagar the Womb were sound checking and having seen these bands play over the last couple of weeks to fill in for the non-arrivals, we told them, 'You ain't on the bill,'—not sure if we were polite about it!" Andy Martin has a tempering perspective: "I do vaguely recall irritation and annoyance from various people at a couple of bands not arriving when they'd been booked to play. I don't state this as fact, merely a suspicion, that what might have happened is someone said they'd ask them to play and the flyers were printed before the bands confirmed their appearance." Simple logistics were also responsible for the Whitehouse cancellation on Saturday 5 June. Though it fell amid this spell of apparent skulduggery, cancellation was down to the far more prosaic reason that the PA didn't turn up.[2]

The large space continued to benefit the Railton Road anarchists who booked a three-day festival for Friday 18–Sunday 20 June: 'Beyond the Bullshit! Festival And Weekend of Action.'

Blood and Roses at the school gate (Courtesy of Erica Echinberg)

Hagar the Womb, Friday 4 June 1982 (Courtesy of Mick Slaughter)

Sequel to conferences held in Oxford in 1980–1981, this iteration was more ambitious and positioned the nature of Centro
Iberico as a core part of its ethos: "The format and the location
is different—less talk, more action, and a squatted building for a
venue.... We hope that EVERYONE will decide to come, wherever
you're based, whether you're an anarchist, anarcho-syndicalist,
anarchist-feminist, libertarian socialist." To the politicised
communities involved, squatting was an act of resistance in and
of itself—García himself was praised posthumously by Meltzer
for being "just as much concerned in helping people to squat in
London."[3]

For total immersion, and the convenience of those travelling,
attendees were invited to bring sleeping bags and crash overnight
in both halls, with meals served on site each evening, and a creche
organised. The Friday saw a performance by Wendy Wattage—the
drag queen persona of Jim Ellis famed for performing on stilts—
with Tony Allen, comedian and organiser of the 'Idiot Ballroom'
events at Meanwhile Gardens, curating the rest of the evening.[4] A
range of talks filled Saturday and Sunday with a two-hour simultaneous picket of various embassies taking place at some point
over the weekend to show solidarity with anarchist prisoners:
the Embassy of Spain just a short distance away in Knightsbridge
presumably received a visit.

The Alternative Centre returned in style the following weekend with UK Decay, Sex Gang Children, and Blood and Roses. This
gathering of bands associated with the emergence of goth fore-
shadowed the launch of the famed Batcave a month later, located
on Dean Street. It was an energy well suited to the old school
with its limited lighting as Kay Byatt noted: "Centro Iberico was
darker than Wapping—physically darker, as well as the feeling
of the place. I remember Blood and Roses playing with all these
candles and skulls on the stage, a real atmosphere. The gigs would
then finish at a certain time, before it got too dark, so you could
all get back home."

UK Decay was the biggest group to perform at Centro Iberico
and arrived off the back of touring in the US, Europe, and across

Hagar the Womb, Friday 4 June 1982 (Courtesy of Mick Slaughter)

YOUTH IN ASIA
BLOOD & ROSES
EMPTY DREAMS

CENTRO IBÉRICO
421 HARROW ROAD
WESTBOURNE PARK
SUNDAY 13TH JUNE ~ 6.30 P.M.

WE DO HOPE TO HAVE THESE BANDS ON

£1

"We do hope to have these bands on," Sunday 13 June 1982 (Courtesy of Kill Your Pet Puppy)

the UK where they had invited support bands like Southern Death Cult and Sisters of Mercy, soon to be stars of the up-and-coming scene.

Steve Spon (UK Decay): We'd done 500 gigs in four years, 150–200 in 1982, a blur of gigs. We'd played a squat in Paris where the anarchist squatters had fallen out so we were told we had to stay in the changing room after the gig because one of the squatters was firing a gun through the doors; one in Berlin on the top floor of an office block overlooking Checkpoint Charlie so we were playing and looking out the windows at tank traps, guard dogs and machine guns! We had the same kind of philosophy to a lot of the Crass and anarchy bands but we were getting a bit psychedelic, proto-goth (though we didn't know it at the time), a lot more fluidity to the guitars, effects, tribalistic drumming and Abbo (Steve Abbott) liked dressing up in costumes. Someone called us "the 1982 fanzine darlings," which is how we met Kill Your Pet Puppy.

Bob Short: We played on the ground floor with an unexpectedly huge PA, there was even foldback which never happened at anarcho-punk gigs.... Going to gigs carrying drums and amps on the bus and tube from Stoke Newington, we tried to play early because it was physically difficult to get back if we finished late—some people thought we just vanished mysteriously!

Andi Sex Gang: There were other squatted places around putting on shows, but I think Centro Iberico was the only one that we ever played and it wasn't like other gigs. You turned up and it wasn't regimented. There was a real communal thing going on. Also, at least I didn't get electrocuted on stage! Anarchism meant no safety laws, no regulations: two nights in Paris for an anarchist radio station with home wiring, I kept getting electrocuted!

Beyond the Bullshit

OVER the last 2 years a conference of (some) anarchists has been held at Oxford. This year the format and the location is different—less talk, more action and a squatted building for a venue.

Brixton Anarchists are organising this 'Beyond the Bullshit' event. They write: 'We hope that EVERYONE will decide to come—wherever you're based, whether you're an anarchist, anarcho-syndicalist, anarchist-feminist, libertarian socialist..etc It's an ideal opportunity for everyone to find out what's been happening—or not— around the country and for people to make new contacts.

We will try and find accommodation for everyone who turns up, but please let us know in advance if you're coming. Phone us on 01-274 6655 or write to us at 121 Railton Road, London SE24. Bring sleeping-bags with you.'

If you've got any ideas about the weekend, then send in the details. A few suggestions for possible discussion topics have already been made. These include—

Civil disturbances/creative vandalism
Squatting and the refusal to pay
Expropriation—exchanging techniques
The Right to Shirk
Pornography, rape and sexism
Fascism, Bolshevism—fighting back
Tape exchange network/media access
Please be specific when offering ideas for discussion.

If you find you're unable to come, but have material to circulate, send it on. If you can come, don't forget to bring with you any locally produced material/reports (including tapes, videos, posters, stickers, badges, etc).

The venue is the Centro Iberico, 421 Harrow Road, London W10 (Westbourne Park tube). The dates are June 18-20 and the festival/weekend will get going between 5-7pm on the Friday. Cheap food will be provided as will some 'entertainment'. Facilities include a self-managed creche. Registration fee of £1 will be payable on the day.

Beyond the Bullshit Festival
(*Freedom* 43, no. 8, 1 May 1982)

BEYOND THE BULLSHIT

Conference/event at
Centro Iberico
421 Harrow Road,
London W10
(Westbourne Park tube)
June 18th, 19th, 20th.

Beyond the Bullshit Festival
(*Freedom* 43, no. 10, 29 May 1982)

conference

18th-20th June. Centro Iberico, 421a Harrow Road, London W10. Here are further details of the Festival/Weekend of Action, outlined below. More information can be obtained from 121 Anarchist Bookshop, 121 Railton Road, Brixton. Tel: 01-274 6655.

Friday 18th
5-8pm arrive and food.
8-11pm music/humour including Wendy Wattage Live, Tony Allen and friends, Psychotics.

Saturday 19th
10-1pm Reports and Workshops.
1-2pm Food.
2-4pm Simultaneous picket of selected embassy in solidarity with anarchist prisoners.

4-8pm Workshop.
8-9pm Meal.
9-12pm Music/humour: Heuristic Music, Anarchist Review, Keith and Robert.

Sunday 20th
10-6pm Discussion, Workshop Food, Video.
It is hoped that everyone will arrive early on Friday as it can be seen that plenty has been laid on. Don't forget to bring reports, papers, publications, videos (VHS only), flags, tapes etc, as well as sleeping bags. Also let us know in advance if you require creche facilities.

Beyond the Bullshit Festival (*Freedom* 43, no. 11, 12 June 1982)

BEYOND THE BULLSHIT!
FESTIVAL AND WEEKEND OF ACTION
(JUNE 18-20 · CENTRO IBERICO · LONDON · WESTBOURNE PARK ⊖

FRIDAY 18TH.
* 5-7P.M. ARRIVE & FOOD.

* 7P.M. "FUN & ACTION" ON THE TOWN.

SATURDAY 19TH.
* 10-6P.M. TALKS/LOCAL REPORTS.
* 6-7P.M. MEAL.
* 7-11P.M. MORE FUN & ACTION & NON-ALIGNED PARTY.

SUNDAY 20TH.
* 10-5P.M. MORE TALKS & VIDEOS
* 5P.M. FOOD.
* 6P.M. EVERYONE GOES ON ABOUT HOW BORING THE WEEKEND WAS.

NOTE: Bring sleeping bags, a sense of humour and plenty of energy. Let us know in advance if you're coming—phone 01-274 6655 or write to The Brixton Anarchists (Beyond the Bullshit!), 121 Books/Anarchist Centre, 121 Railton Road, London SE24.. Also send in ideas for discussion topics. Suggestions already made include— Civil disturbances/creative vandalism; Squatting and the refusal to pay ; Expropriation - exchanging techniques ; The Right to Shirk; Pornography, rape and sexism; Fascism and Bolshevism—fighting back; Tape exchange/media access. See ya!

Beyond the Bullshit Festival, Friday 18 through Sunday 20 June

BEYOND THE ROLE PLAY

Hello FREEDOM!
Just like to add my comments on the recent Beyond the Bullshit Conference.

I had hoped I was to take part in a creative and inspiring event that would spark off new ideas and new enthusiasm. The sick reality of it all was a bit different. I found I was in the presence of some of the most depressed, bored, apathetic, deflating and totally negative people I had ever come across. Rather than the conference being a forum for action and imagination it was used as chance to moan about how awful, cretinous and abismal everything was and how everyone that was actually trying to do anything was wasting their time and how nothing was ever going to change. People seemed more intent on watching video after video of various riots/street battles and assorted other carnage than on discussing anything worthwhile.

But I think the most revealing aspect of the whole weekend was the total lack of self-awareness of most of the people present — one guy who suggested we should go and attack Macdonalds, presumably in protest to their mass trade in dead animal, was wearing: a leather jacket, covered in nice macho studs, a leather belt with more studs and leather DMs complete with further studs! What can

you say? The hypocrisy is so glaringly obvious. Similarly, many of the girls present, who had supposedly rejected society's right to control them had masses of make up on, preened hair and the 'latest' chic clothing — PURE ROLE PLAY. It's no good going out to change/ smash the system if you can't even change yourself. We've got to face up to this — at an anarchist conference the workshops were dominated by the largest, loudest males who shoved their ideas to the exclusion of all else.

It is painfully obvious that within the anarchist/libertarian movement people continue to be unaware of themselves and the way they relate to others. The survival of the war machine depends on BIG MAN BIG M.A.N. with subservient wo-man in tow — change that IT'S IN THE MIRROR THAT THE REAL WAR STARTS.
Anarchy + liberty,
RICHARD CROSS

Beyond the Bullshit Festival (*Freedom* 43, no. 13, 10 July 1982)

Sex Gang Children, Blood and
Roses, and UK Decay, Saturday
26 June (Courtesy of Mickey
Penguin)

"Do what thou wilt shall
be the whole of the law,"
Saturday 26 June (Courtesy of
Mickey Penguin)

Liberated from a wall outside
Westbourne Park Underground
(Courtesy of Michael Clarke)

"Love Is The Law, Love Under Will,"
Sunday 13 and Saturday 26 June

Richard Cabut from the group Brigandage took on responsibility for working the door and was in the unusual position of
sharing duties with UK Decay's own people and having to make
his friends pay when they were used to walking in free.

Tony Drayton: There was no guest list so they couldn't
blag their way in and I wound up having to pay the 50p for
certain people. UK Decay were a proper band and they'd
bought a big van with all their equipment so, understand-
ably, they expected to get paid while bands like Blood and
Roses were just happy to play and if you got them some
money, fine. Truth is we never had any takings. We'd just
hand it to the bands. Sex Gang Children were great, this
very theatrical and decadent 'pre-goth but goth event.' UK
Decay had a lot of followers down from Luton who weren't
normal 'anarchy centre people' and graffitied "Luton FC" all
over my pyramid! The gig wiped us out a bit, just left us too
exhausted to put stuff on for a week or two.

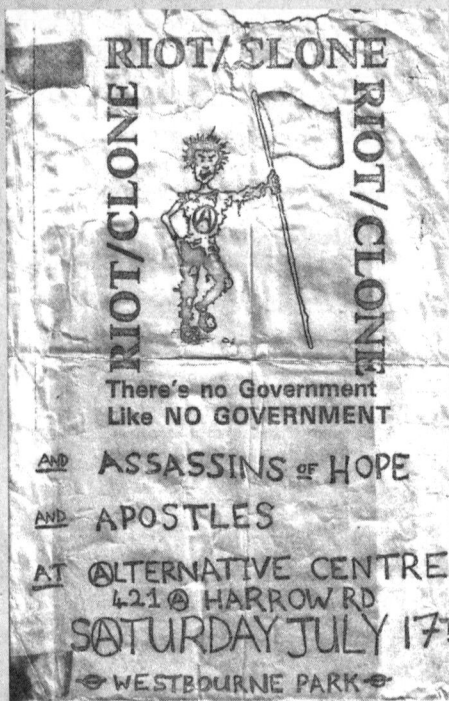

Riot/Clone, Assassins of Hope, and The Apostles, Saturday 17 July (Courtesy of Kill Your Pet Puppy)

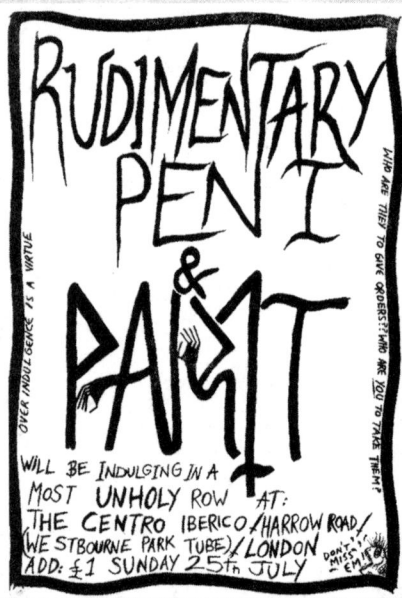

Rudimentary Peni, Part One, and Faction, Sunday 25 July (Courtesy of Kill Your Pet Puppy)

MOBS, POETS, SINYX, AND WINDMILLS

Having supported the festival, activity at Centro Iberico seems to have paused for two weekends. After the breather, there was a gentle rekindling with old favourites returning—Assassins of Hope and The Apostles (17 July); Rudimentary Peni and Part One (25 July)—and newcomers welcomed in—Riot/Clone on the 17 July, Faction on 25 July.

Comfortable in the home they'd created, during the summer gig-goers would often spill out into the playground and bask in the summer sun. Tony Drayton: "It was a natural progression once we were on the ground floor: the bands would be inside while people would be hanging around outside. It's a crucial point: this wasn't just a gig venue for us, it was a social venue where people gathered and maybe wouldn't even go into the gig, hanging out was just as important. There was a regular hard core of about thirty, then 100–150 people coming for the bands. With a whole bunch of punks walking down the street and then shouting in the playground the locals kept a bit of distance!"

Stiflingly hot in the summer, the old school hosted The Mob and The Sinyx for a sweaty and uncomfortable show on Sunday 1 August. As had happened at the Throbbing Gristle show in 1979, the climatic conditions enhanced the potency of the experience for those able to endure it. The night started with a couple of impromptu moments. First, Tony Drayton, Richard Cabut, and his girlfriend Jo performed as Windy Miller and the Windmills using The Mob's equipment. Second, a friend of The Sinyx, Giacomino Parkinson, "read or ranted poetry, inspired by the fact that this type of performance seemed to work—I had seen John Cooper

The Sinyx,
Sunday
1 August
(Courtesy of
Steve Pegrum
and Angels in
Exile Records
Archive)

Clarke. It was a friendly place, no trouble, the audience gave me a listen and good feedback."

> **Steve Pegrum:** I remember the haze of a late summer's afternoon, unloading the equipment from the van—Mark from The Mob and everyone else helped—and walking it into the space where people had painted the walls in interesting ways with an astounding array of colours. I remember having a great feeling about the place and the gig. It was a sweltering August night and it was rammed. A couple of friends of ours took photos and Giacomino jumped on stage and read a couple of his poems. The audience was really into it. It was really hot, so intense, before the encore I had to vomit and then I temporarily passed out before just making it back for 'Fight,' our encore. Our songs had a kind of tribal intensity to them which would be simultaneously very draining and very uplifting to play. After we played I felt euphoric—and quite shattered too! The Mob then played a great set and it ended the night on a high.

Now six months in residence at Harrow Road, two months longer than they'd lasted at Wapping, perhaps it was inevitable that conflict would arise as the small community organising the Alternative Centre grew increasingly exhausted while remaining divided into two distinct camps. Friday 13 August's appearance by The Apostles, Omega Tribe, Riot/Clone, Icons of Filth, and Conflict seems to have brought everything to a head. As Tony Drayton recalled: "The Conflict gig was meant to be Andy's retort to the supposed decadence of the UK Decay gig. After that UK Decay/Sex Gang Children evening, Andy froze us Puppies out so I wasn't at the Conflict gig as I was persona non grata."

There's a well-known story in which Andy Martin and Ian Slaughter—creator of the *Pigs for Slaughter* fanzine—made strenuous efforts to turn the hot air of anarchism on the dancefloor, into anarchy on the warm summer streets. As Martin wrote in his widely circulated account:

LONDON. Centro Iberico, Conflict

Conflict gig, Friday 13 August (*Sounds*, 14 August 1982)

Conflict, Friday 13 August 1982 (Courtesy of Chris Low)

The Apostles, Friday 13 August 1982 (Courtesy of Chris Low)

Ian telephoned the local police to say that trouble was
about to erupt at that damned squatted school, would they
come along with shields and truncheons, please? By the
end of Conflict's set, I'd succeeded in the arousal of two
hundred angry, frustrated punks and skinheads.... At Ian's
signal, they rushed toward the stairwell which led down
to the playground.... I led from the front but by the time
I rushed out into the cold night air, I'd lost two-thirds of
my battalion; by the time I reached the front gates, three-
quarters of the remaining platoon had vanished. Ian was
so furious that he hurled a house brick at a police van
that happened to pass. One of the policemen glanced out
the window briefly then turned his gaze back to the road
ahead. As the punks sauntered merrily off down the road,
Ian grabbed individuals at random: "Come on, fight! We
can smash shop windows, wreck the town!" One young lad
replied (and these are his exact words), "No, sorry, I have
to go to work tomorrow."[1]

While compellingly written, the tale isn't to be taken liter-
ally; it's more a dream vision expressing honest dissatisfaction
with the gap between lyrical claims versus the passive reality
of consumer culture in gig form. In 'Communique 8' the Angry
Brigade suggested, "blow it up or burn it down.... You can't
reform profit capitalism and inhumanity. Just kick it till it breaks."
The phrase resonated in anarcho-punk circles, providing the title
for an Apostles' EP in 1983 and paraphrased for the border of
"Why Punk Is a Total Failure," a flyer Slaughter was handing out
at gigs which declaimed: "Those who need to fall back upon a set
of lyrics or painted leather jackets to prop themselves up will not
survive.... Those who are willing to challenge the state, to work
for its downfall, these are the ones who can earn the right to call
themselves anarchists."

Hugh Vivian: The drugs of choice that night were alcohol
and glue. I remember the singer from The Apostles singing,

Omega Tribe, Friday 13 August 1982 (Courtesy of Chris Low)

Icons of Filth, Friday 13 August 1982
(Courtesy of Chris Low)

Subhumans, The Mob, A Heads,
and Pagans, Sunday 22 August

"What are we doing here? We're all just fucking queer!" He seemed quite upset about that. When Conflict were on stage people were doing that very aggressive dancing where you grab hold of someone's jacket and wrestle them about consensually—I've never really been into that!

A recording of The Apostles' performance exists featuring, 'Fucking Queer.' The song's vitriol against the omnipresent homophobia of the era was converted into a lash whipped across the back of those in the room with Martin introducing the song: "This one's called 'Fucking Queer.' It's for ... [laughs] ... It's for everyone." Amid the lo-fi murk, one can hear the chorus, "What are you doing here? You're all just fucking queer! What am I doing here? I'm just fucking queer! What are we doing here? We're all just fucking queer!" John Soares (aka John Apostle) also tells the crowd: "this is for all the people who think it's fucking enough to put an 'A' in a circle on their jackets. You make me fucking sick!" to the appropriate retort of a cheery round of applause.[2]

A piece by Chris Low in the book *Not Just Bits of Paper*, explains: "For some unfathomable reason they had a succession of different drummers, could they have been too scared to spend too long sharing the stage with Andy Martin? He did seem very angry about something.... Andy got more irascible with every song and, perhaps so he'd avoid the veins in his neck exploding, vocal duties for the last two numbers were consigned to other band members leaving Andy to concentrate on playing his guitar like Lou Reed and exuding rancour." Low confirms, "Icons of Filth were the final band to play but I only caught a couple of songs before having to leave to run for the last tube." It's unlikely a significant number of people were coaxed from the room before the final band, even if some needed to leave for practical reasons."[3]

No one mentions a mass exodus of practically the entire room or the drama of a riot at the end of the playground. The original text located the gig up on a nonexistent 'fourth floor,' when the gig clearly took place on the ground floor so there would be no dramatic rush of bodies down the stairwell. And, of course, losing the best part of two hundred troops between the gymnasium and the school door, a distance of barely a few feet, is the same as saying no one had moved an inch. In all likelihood, if anything happened at all, it was just Martin and Slaughter stood out on the Harrow Road imagining the police van and the brick. Instead, the story stands as a glorious fantasia in which the possibility of anarchist revolt dissipates on contact with reality.

THE END

Everyone knew it couldn't last forever.

Though two further Alternative Centre gigs followed on Saturday 14 August and Sunday 22 August 1982, it seems the energy needed for recruiting bands, broadcasting them through word-of-mouth networks, arriving early to set up, running rather than watching the show, then staying late to clear up... That reserve of energy evaporated in the summer heat.

Andy Martin: I have the impression that the punk bands, pop groups, poets, and assorted weirdos departed after that leaving the Spanish anarchists behind.

Tony Drayton: I think that might have been Andy's last event because Conflict brought their own people to run the door and he was having to tell his friends that they had to pay too. Meanwhile, we just fizzled out. There were lots of new venues happening in Central London, places like the Batcave, and it had been so much effort, it was time to stop.

Phil Barker: There was a change in the attitude and the people. After Wapping, the early unity seemed to have gone and sides were being taken... while still working together to a point. People all over the country were squatting and doing stuff so it started to go public as some were now music journalists. It became more about the music and the bands, coupled with the hippy crossover of Stonehenge, the New Age Travellers—and drugs. It was more ramshackle,

**The Mob, Sunday 22 August 1982
(Courtesy of Mark Wilson)**

more chaotic, and a little cliquey. After Centro Iberico, the scene fragmented and people grew up.... People changed.... Some people just carried on—bottles of cider, glue, long hair, squatty, trampy, poverty-stricken.

On Saturday 11 September, Nigel Jacklin's experimental project, Alien Brains, played the venue. Jacklin, who had seen Whitehouse perform at the school, strolled in one day and asked the Spanish squatters if he and his friends could play. Despite a mention in *Sounds*, there was no joyously frenzied mass of a hundred or more anarcho-punks, barely anyone at all. A small posse did show up including Steven Stapleton and John Fothergill of Nurse with Wound, along with Ralf Wehowsky—a founding member of experimental group P16.D4.

Nigel Jacklin (Alien Brains): The line-up was myself, Philip and Richard Rupenus, Philip Sanderson, and Neal Purvis. We carried our equipment from where I lived off Portobello Road and stopped for a drink at the Frog and Firkin pub. I picked up a scaffold pole on the way and that was my main instrument. It was quiet and pretty empty. The downstairs area where we played was large, dark, and damp. A bit dusty. I didn't care whether anyone turned up—though maybe a couple of people did—because it wasn't about the audience, it was about playing. Squats and empty, semi-derelict buildings were not unusual at the time. We played the derelict Victorian baths on Lancaster Road and, by comparison, Centro Iberico was luxury! The baths had broken glass everywhere and you could only get in by climbing through a small window. Centro Iberico at least had a door.

At some point in late summer, the straight world intruded into Centro Iberico's liberated zone.

Eduardo Niebla: We weren't properly equipped to live there, we didn't have running water, we didn't have a phone,

LONDON. Centro Iberico, Harrow Road, Eduardo A
Niebla Quintet

Eduardo Niebla Quartet, Saturday 21 August (*Sounds*, 21 August 1982)

LONDON, Centro Iberico, Harrow Road. Nigel
Jacklin/Alien Brains/Bladder Flask

Alien Brains, Saturday 11 September (*Sounds*, 11 September 1982)

Nigel Jacklin and Philip Rupenus enter Centro Iberico (Courtesy of Richard Rupenus)

the other side of the building was derelict while where we were just looked old, like it needed looking after. We were always aware that someday we would need to leave. Out of the blue, a guy came from the council with an eviction order and we had to go to court. We basically went for nothing, we knew we didn't stand a chance; it wasn't our place and they could do whatever they wanted with it.

William Orbit: The council never bothered us at Harrow Road: squatting was more acceptable and the councils wanted squatters in because it meant someone was looking after the place. Sometimes letters would come saying, "We're going to pull it down. You're going to have to move out," but they never did.... Until, obviously, eventually, they did. The final threat came and we took it seriously and found a place up in Little Venice. They called our bluff because it was a little while longer before they rendered it rubble.

Torch Song exited the cottage and headed to Little Venice with Rico Conning believing the move took place in October. Meanwhile, following an initial court date in November, the Spanish occupants prepared a festival intended to raise funds for legal action but which ultimately served as a grand farewell. Across Friday 3 to Sunday 5 December, more than twenty different performers took the stage presenting everything from piano jazz to flamenco guitar, poetry to comedy, even Blanca Bartos of the Musa Oxoniensis/Musa Iberica group performing what is listed on the poster as 'medieval music.'

Many of the anarcho-punk contingent would grace the area, though not the school itself, on Saturday 18 December. The now-empty Zig Zag Club was squatted for an all-day event as Penny Rimbaud recounts: "We told everyone it was going to be the Rainbow so that all the pressure from the authorities was on there, meaning the Zig Zag was unwatched and we could move in and announce it a day before. We had all sorts of funny codes

LIVERPOOL, Klub Fiasco, Warehouse, Fleet Street, (051 709 1530), Sinatras

LLANDUDNO, Astra Cinema, (76666), Gary Moore ~Band

LONDON, Ad Lib, Kensington, Russell Gardens, (01-603 3245), Recruits/Blood Oranges

LONDON, Albany Empire, Douglas Way, (01-691 8016), Rico/The Breakfast Band

LONDON, Barbican Centre, (01-638 8891), Body And Soul (lunchtime)

LONDON, The Cellar, Cecil Sharp House, Chris Rohmann

LONDON, Centro Iberico, Harrow Road, Andy Mason Units And The Ffuts/Closer To The Sun

LONDON, Centro Iberico, Harrow Road, Andy Mason Units And The Ffuts/Closer To The Sun

LONDON, Dingwalls, Camden Lock, (01-267 4967), Billy Connolly/Malcolm The Magician

LONDON, Dominion, Tottenham Court Road, (01-580 9562), Shalamar

LONDON, Dublin Castle, Camden, (01-485 1773), Swamp Creatures (lunchtime) Zodiacs (evening)

*LONDON, Hammersmith Odeon, (01-748 4081), Ultravox

LONDON, Hog's Grunt, Production Village, Cricklewood, (01-450 8969), Peter Neighbour (lunchtime) Snacks At The Bar (evening)

LONDON, Lewisham Concert Hall, (01-690 3431), Three

The Farewell Festival, Friday 3 through Sunday 5 December (*Sounds*, 4 December 1982)

The final flyer for Centro Iberico (Courtesy of Eduardo Niebla)

so we could keep it a tight secret until we were settled in and ready to go." Omega Tribe, Lack of Knowledge, Sleeping Dogs, Faction, The Apostles, Youth in Asia, Polemic, Amebix, Null and Void, The Mob, Poison Girls, Conflict, Flux of Pink Indians, Crass, and DIRT—the Zig Zag squatting was a coming together of many veterans of the Autonomy Centre and Alternative Centre, a last hurrah for all three venues.

On 21 February 1983, lawyers for the Brent People's Housing Association were busy submitting applications for the execution of works related to new housing. Eduardo Niebla remembers: "My understanding is that the man from the council had purchased the building from the council with the argument that he was going to build flats for the poor. In the end, whatever he built, they were not cheap and he made a lot of money. When they were preparing to evict us, the first thing that happened was some guys came in with trucks and they took the parquet flooring because it was original and potentially very expensive."

In the absence of García's indomitable will, vacation not just of the site but of the entire vision of a 'Centro Iberico' was unsurprising. A bulletin in *Black Flag* in early March 1983 read last rites: "After seven years occupation the Centro Iberico in Harrow Road, West London, is to be evicted in a month's time. They are now looking for new premises (squatted or otherwise) in the West London area, and people with energy to help with the move itself should turn up." Though the notice contained a hint of hope that something new might arise, no one pressed for Centro Iberico's survival. Niebla observed the aftermath: "Everyone went to different houses—I didn't wait for the very end.... For a time, a few of us would meet up but everyone lost contact as quite a few of the guys moved back to Spain."

Even at such a late hour, there was perhaps one last encore for the old school. In an article, Al Puppy speaks of a Sunday in 1983, "Walking up past the still empty Zig Zag club … I remembered the weekend in December it had been squatted.… Still smiling I turned the corner and walked down Harrow Road to the Centro Iberico.… Inside are a few Spanish people, clearing out the last of

PUNK LIVES
IN THE STRANGEST PLACES

Al A, one of the writers for the 'Kill Your Pet Puppy' fanzine explains what punk means to him and reports on the Harrow Road Anarchy Centre's final gig

WHEN THE first twitches of what was to become punk started seeping out of London and into the world, the first trickle of interested parties started hitching their way towards the city. As the twitches got stronger, the weirdos kept coming, crawling in from all over the UK, even places like Australia and America.

KINGS CROSS

IN EARLY '79, large areas of Kings Cross were taken over by punk squatters. "Police vans used to turn up every morning to haul away anyone who looked underage. Some people had to carry a birth certificate all the time.

"I used to sleep in the empty carriages at Euston Station.

"I was on the tube and this girl said 'Do you want to buy some blues?' I didn't know what they were, but me and my mate bought a quid's worth. We used to be speeding all night down the Music Machine and sleep on the circle line and abuse the commuters.

"We used to go and swop joints and downers for cider and meths with the dossers."

"WHEN YOU'VE BEEN UP FOR FIVE DAYS" . . .

ENERGY is not always eternal delight; eventually you come down and it doesn't seem so much fun. Being worried. Being arrested. Being beaten up. Overdoses. Having to beg. And meanwhile the original fragile unity of punk was splitting up into a hundred fragments under the onslaughts of the media and society. The Tories got elected. The elements of punk's initial energy — Sexual, political, musical, fashion, drugs; lost touch with each other and became impotent gestures. Only the fact of punk's very success in "speaking for a generation" gave any credibility to the post punk morass. A succession of "spokesmen" tried to use the impetus of punk to push their careers and opinionated ideas. "Punk is dead".

PUNK IS DEAD?

ALMOST, BUT not quite. Some of those who had made the trek to London didn't go back home, couldn't go back home. Back to the situation as before. They had found a freedom in the city, in punk, however fragile and insecure. There was no going back to Middlesborough, or Sydney or Cumberland or . . . They had crossed over into the Abyss. The only question was, would they ever reach the other side?

ANTS/TUINAL/CRASS

THE HEADING from a fanzine of January 1980 summed it all up. The old Ants and their links with the old spirit of punk (and the whole glam era which has warped the minds of this generation back in 72/73), the old Ants were beginning the metamorphosis from decadent punk to teen glamour. The speed was being replaced by drugs like Tuinal.

"More and more people were saying 'I can take tuinal without being addicted'.

"You'd see them staggering about, oblivious to anyone or anything, 'another generation goes down kicking and screaming . . .'.

"Some of our best friends have turned into aggressive, destructive bastards through this drug, which suddenly flooded the market when a number of amphetamine factories got busted."

The only glimmer of hope was in Crass, a heavy anarchist punk band with the image and ideals for the moment. At the gigs throughout 1979 the splinters of punk clashed in ugly confrontation. The winter of 79/80 had been the coldest on record. It seemed like a long way from the summer of '76.

PERSON'S UNKNOWN

1979 ALSO saw the "Anarchist Conspiracy Trial" and the spark of inspiration which became the London Anarchist Centre. A series of meetings were held in late '79 early '80; perhaps there was more to 'Anarchy In The UK' than just a song. Maybe it could HAPPEN!

In April, Crass and the Poison Girls became involved. There was a single. There was money. Not much else.

1980

WHAT WAS there? Bauhaus, the Cramps and the Psychedelic Furs: Music without morals. Crass: Morals without music. A crowded, colourful anarchist picnic on Mayday. Lots of punks! But nothing much on the surface, a deceptive calm.

1981

THE PACE began to quicken. A nervous energy (or was it the speed?).

More gigs. More people. Riots. Obviously something was going on, not always pleasant, a violent tinge to events.

A PARALLEL UNIVERSE

SUDDENLY, SOMEHOW, things changed. Gigs in a church, a squat on the Pentonville Road, No bouncers, no more "them" and "us". 50p to see bands like Rubella Ballet the Synix and Tinsel jumping up to sing with them. Gigs organised by punks, for punks. Not safe punks in mail order leather jackets. No, this lot were still outrageous, gay punks living in squats, anarchist punks with dazzlingly bright hair and make up. The survivors, the ones who had passed through the abyss. And now they were finding each other again, discovering a network of people and bands and squats and fanzines. A Blood and Roses gig in Stoke Newington. Sitting in a room in an Islington squat, waiting for the dawn, and a free gig at Parliament Hill Fields, sunshine, laughter and the Entire Cosmos plus the Mob and King Trigger.

It was all very confusing, so much seemed to be happening, so much was happening. The Wild Youth were on the streets again, a kaleidoscopic frenzy, a celebration. It is true — PUNK LIVES!

WAPPING

IN THE meantime the real anarchists were getting on with the Anarchy Centre in Wapping. It ended up in a sad state. But there their new confidence the punks managed to keep it going — all through another freezing winter. The church had moved east (due to a fire). More coming together, more people, more friends.

1982

WE CELEBRATED the new year with an all night concert/celebration. Three years on and the pieces were coming together again, expanding slowly. Then we got evicted. The spirit moved west to the Centro Iberica, the mood changing from the cold aggressive mood of Wapping to a more relaxed and sensual feel. A psychedelic slant to the old punk rant. The militants

RUBELLA BALLET: only 50p to see them play

Al Puppy (aka Alistair Livingston)'s last Iberico tale (Courtesy of Kill Your Pet Puppy)

were wary — all this enjoyment — was this the revolution?

Of course it is, complete with candles and magick, crazy colour and chaos. Only this time we are singing the songs (thanks Brigandage).

And on the fringes, hiding in the toilets, the journalists and film crews. Jo Brocklehurst's paintings have captured the flamboyant style, but will they grasp the content? Or will they just grab the cliches like before?

INTO THE OPEN

WHAT HAPPENS when we wake from our three years slumber? When they start to uncover the hidden growth? When you see it in the papers, watch it on TV? Wobbling on the edge, is there enough control, or will it be lost again? Punk is alive, the only subversive thing around, the only real threat left.

The police vans still turn up every morning to haul away the underagers. Only now it's glue, not tuinal.

Does anyone grasp the implications? Punk lives in the places Gary Bushell has never been. We've crossed the abyss, but will anyone follow?

Are you tired of all these questions? Then it's time to find some answers of your own!

IT WAS late on Friday night, and I was half asleep when Dave came round with the news.

"There is going to be a free gig at London's Anarchy Centre, the last one before they knock it down."

"Great, who's playing?"

"The Mob and Null and Void. A P.A. has been hired for Sunday."

"This Sunday?"

"Yeah."

He disappeared off into the night to carry the word. I had a cig and fell asleep. I dreamt that a TV crew came round to film the event and no one turned up. That would be typical Anarchy Centre style.

I arrived about 4.30 on Sunday, walking up past the still empty Zig Zag club. It looked the same, but I remembered the weekend in December it had been squatted in. That was great, especially the free beer! Still smiling I turned the corner and walked down Harrow Road to the Centro Iberico, where the A Centre has been for the past year.

It is in a huge empty school, hidden behind advertising hoardings. The entrance is a creaky iron gate labelled "Girls". It groaned as I pushed it open. Just like in a Mob song "the playground is empty", the half ruined school is like a haunted house. The ground floor windows are covered with wire mesh. Painted letters spell out CENTRO IBERICO and an arrow points to a small door. I can hear music from inside, so someone must be in.

Inside are a few Spanish people, clearing out the last of their belongings. I wander round the tiny stage in 'our' part — it is built from old gas cookers, classroom doors and a lump of carpet salvaged from a skip. The lights came from the old Wapping A Centre, the only relics left. The walls are all painted, some pictures, some slogans. It is all very forlorn and sad, but I still have the memories.

Goes back to the infamous summer of '81. When assorted members of the 'Pet Puppy' fanzine's collective went to the Hope and Anchor. Some of us stayed, the others went in search of a 'church' where you could see all these punk bands for 50p. They returned the next afternoon, full of this church — a squat on the Pentonville Road, and a gay punk squat. Both places were to become familiar over the next

Centro Iberico: last home of the Anarchy Centre

Open to all

The stage, built from old cookers and classroom doors

months.

Things were happening so fast then, it's hard to recall much more than flashes; a glimpse of Rubella Ballet — who are these amazing people? Suddenly there was this tiny church full of the most wierd, bizarre punks, all (nearly) being friendly and relaxed. No bouncer, no management, no bar, no rules!

Unfortunately it eventually caught fire, I saw it the other day from the bus, all boarded up and looking like it came out of an H.P. Lovecraft story. Still in the depths of darkest Wapping was a warehouse — the original Autonomy/Anarchy Centre, set up with the help of the money from the Bloody Revolutions/Persons Unknown single.

It was losing money, so And-ee Martin who opened the place for punks on Sunday, set up some benefit gigs. A new church, just a bit colder now — it was November! People would arrive in the afternoon and huddle together for warmth until there were enough bodies to take the edge off the cold air.

Over the months though, things got 'spontaneously' organised — like tea and coffee, veggie food and lager at 50p a can (I helped on this one!). Fanzines and anarchic literature were sold and blues bought; the talk got so fast and furious while the bands played on. Six or seven bands a night is good value for a pound. We celebrated New Year there and almost froze to death in a blizzard!

Unfortunately the landlord found out about our fun and threw us out.

And so to the Centro Iberico where the chaos continued, but on a slightly larger scale. Not so cold either. Scattered groups of punks in the playground, clutching the inevitable bottles of cider (sweet and dry), gossiping and laughing, waiting for the band or the equipment to arrive. Usually it would get sorted out after a series of frantic phone calls. More relaxed than Wapping, the styles a bit wilder, the music a bit broader — expanding the boundaries of punk.

And here we are again, going out in style with Fracture, The Omega Tribe, Null and Void and The Mob. I talk too much and miss most of the bands but in the distance I hear the Mob's musical motif, Curtis, tuning his bass. I push through the crowd (who said no one would come?) towards the stage. Oooooh.

Not many bands have that emotional intensity, that real power behind the songs. Blood and Roses have it. The Mob definitely have it. I danced until it ripped my T-shirt to shreds, singing along to all the songs. This is punk rock, this passion and intensity, this compassion and truth. It went on and on — so late I had to walk the last couple of miles home. Even then I couldn't sleep.

I still can't. I have to sit here and try and express it in words, to communicate. What we have done, what we are doing is important, is vital because . . . well since punk began it hasn't got any easier, the collapse of this country has continued and looks like it will continue, despite politicians promises and all those other lies. I saw The Truth Game on TV. The news came on and I found Channel Four — The Birthday Party in full manic majesty. I hadn't much liked them before but in the midst of the horror of today they seemed so right.

Flowers in the Dustbin? The whole nation is becoming a dustbin and the flowers have spread, growing in the rubble. How many young people have a future? Workers aren't needed any more, only machines to make video games and Cruise missiles.

Punk is/was prophetic — all the words are coming true, we have no future in this wasteland. The Anarchy Centre was just a way of showing that it is possible to create our own lives, to live our own lives. Listening to a tape of Blood and Roses, a bit of Tony D.'s drunken interview with Bob.

"They can exploit me. They can exploit the band. BUT THEY CAN NEVER EXPLOIT THE IDEA."

And that is true.

AL A

CENTRO IBERICO TO BE EVICTED

After 7 years occupation the Centro Iberico in Harro Road West London is to be evicted in a months time. They are now looking for new premises (squatted or other-wise) in the West London Area, and people with energy to help with the move itself should turn up at 429 Harrow Road W.London W9.

The end of the Centro Iberico and Harrow Road (*Black Flag* VII, no. 2a, 1983)

their belongings." Though undated, Al describes a decent crowd, "going out in style with Fracture, The Omega Tribe, Null and Void, and The Mob." But this may be another literary mirage because no one else recalls the occasion. While possibly true, it's just as likely this was wish fulfilment, a desire to say a written farewell to a good moment, a good place. Against the claims of a large crowd, there's a tumbleweed silence, not a whisper of memory.

Niebla confirms the building was standing well over a year later, while Mayer visited the area sometime in the mid-1980s to find the caretaker's cottage had survived even longer—Orbit wonders if the cottage was taken over by the woodyard and kept as an office or storage space. On Friday 30 March 1984, Ken Livingstone, leader of the Greater London Council, arrived at the site to attend the official opening of works on the site with the intention being to create thirty-nine homes including ten flats converted for the disabled, ten for single people, and eighteen for families. Further correspondence in April–May 1984, finds the housing association and the City of Westminster going back and forth about condemning the sewers suggesting work was still developing but every indication is it was completed on schedule in summer 1985.[1]

Tom Vague, creator of *Vague* zine, recalls squatting with veterans of Centro Iberico at some point in 1983–1984. Meanwhile, members of The Mob, Kill Your Pet Puppy, allies including Andy Palmer of Crass and Bob Short of Blood and Roses—with significant inspiration from Andy Martin—banded together to run the Black Sheep Housing Co-operative to which Islington Council granted occupation of four houses. The co-op would provide short-term affordable rents to people in need, helping numerous artists and activists to establish and maintain stable lives.[2]

Beyond that, despite the multiple lives it lived across London in the 70s; despite the second life it gave to the stragglers from Wapping; the centre would see no fresh resurrection. The Centro Iberico of Miguel J.M. García García entered history at 421a Harrow Road.

GIGOGRAPHIES

1982 'ALTERNATIVE CENTRE' RESIDENCY AT CENTRO IBERICO

Weekend No.	Date	Bands	Notes and Source for the Event or Gig
0	*Unknown* Last week of February/first week of March	N/A	KYPP Note: "Within two weeks we had the use of a couple of rooms in a Spanish anarchist squat. The first meeting was beautifully chaotic: no equipment, no bands, and about 20 people—just like the old days. We improvised tribal percussion with pieces of wood, cider bottles and lager cans—a chant, 'we shall live again.' Slowly, we did."
1	Friday 5 March	The Mob Zounds Null and Void Youth in Asia	Flyer exists
1	Sunday 7 March	Blood and Roses Flack Empty Dreams	First forthcoming gigs flyer from KYPP
2	Sunday 14 March	Rudimentary Peni Part One	First forthcoming gigs flyer from KYPP
3	Sunday 21 March	12 Cubic Feet The Apostles Lack of Knowledge Vertical Hold Dead Souls Blood and Roses The Replaceable Headz The Cult of the Supreme Being	Flyer exists as well as the second forthcoming gigs flyer from KYPP A gig listing was included with The Apostles' second EP in 1983 which also listed Blood and Roses, The Replaceable Headz and The Cult of the Supreme Being
4	Sunday 28 March	Rubella Ballet Action Pact Dead Man's Shadow	Second forthcoming gigs flyer from KYPP
5	Sunday 4 April	Subhumans Organised Chaos Locusts Hagar the Womb A-Heads	Second forthcoming gigs flyer from KYPP, Sean Forbes has a cassette recording of A-Heads

Weekend No.	Date	Bands	Notes and Source for the Event or Gig
6	Sunday 11 April	Poetry and film evening	Confirmed by Andy Martin
7	Saturday 17 April	DIRT Youth in Asia Heir Attack Burnt Thighs	Paul May from Final Curtain's list of gigs he attended plus Mick Slaughter's bootleg tape list
7	Sunday 18 April	Flux of Pink Indians Cold War Screaming Babies Turd Burglars	Second forthcoming gigs flyer from KYPP KYPP Note: "You could have seen the Turd Burglars at the Alternative Centre, London, with Screaming Babies + Flux of Pink Indians—Not So Brave Without A Banner" ("Not so brave without a banner" was a commentary on Flux having their banner stolen)
8	Sunday 25 April	The Mob Bikini Mutants D-Notice	Second forthcoming gigs flyer from KYPP
9	Saturday 1 May	Whitehouse Neo Naturists	100 strong audience
9	Sunday 2 May	Rubella Ballet Conflict The Apostles Assassins of Hope Amsterdamned	Flyer exists 400 strong audience
10	Sunday 9 May		
11	Sunday 16 May	Gerry Fitzgerald/ Lol Coxhill/Ronnie Watham/Phil Shepherd/Gilli Smythe/Daevid Allen/Lady June	Flyer exists Released as a 1982 cassette on Ottersongs, a tape label run by Harry Williamson whose group supported Lady June on the night
12	Friday 21 May	(Cancelled) Conflict	Some variation of The Apostles, Assassins of Hope, or Hagar the Womb played
13	Friday 28 May	(Cancelled) Flux of Pink Indians	Some variation of The Apostles, Assassins of Hope, or Hagar the Womb played
14	Friday 4 June	DIRT Anthrax Heir Attack Hagar the Womb Omega Tribe	Two flyers exist and an advert in *Sounds* for 5th June 1982 Mick Slaughter confirmed Hagar the Womb Paul May confirmed Omega Tribe from his 1982 gig list

Weekend No.	Date	Bands	Notes and Source for the Event or Gig
14	Saturday 5 June	(Cancelled) Whitehouse Neo-Naturist Cabaret	Advert in *Sounds*, 5 June 1982
15	Saturday 12 June	Whitehouse Neo-Naturist Cabaret Consumer Electronics	Advert in *Sounds*, 12 June 1982 but only mentions Whitehouse and Neo-Naturists
15	Sunday 13 June	Blood and Roses Youth in Asia Empty Dreams Hagar the Womb	Flyer exists, Hagar the Womb confirmed by Mick Slaughter
16	Friday 18 June through Sunday 20 June	Beyond the Bullshit Festival and Weekend of Action	Flyer exists
17	Saturday 26 June	Blood and Roses Sex Gang Children UK Decay	Three flyers exist
18	Sunday 4 July		
19	Sunday 11 July		
20	Saturday 17 July	Riot/Clone Assassins Of Hope The Apostles	Flyer exists
21	Sunday 25 July	Rudimentary Peni Part One Faction	Flyer exists but only mentions Rudimentary Peni and Part One. Faction are included on Paul May of Final Curtain's gig attendance list
22	Sunday 1 August	The Mob The Sinyx Windy Miller and the Windmills Giacomino Parkinson	Photos exist and event confirmed by participating bands
23	Sunday 8 August	Faction	Confirmed by a tape in the possession of Sean Forbes
24	Friday 13 August	The Apostles Conflict The Omega Tribe Riot/Clone Icons of Filth	Advert in *Sounds*, 14 August 1982 only mentions Conflict
24	Saturday 14 August	Assassins of Hope Shreek Riot/Clone The Vicious Hamsters	Confirmed by Chantal Davey's diary and by Riot/Clone, though the latter believe Omega Tribe may have played or been intended to play
25	Saturday 21 August	Eduardo A. Niebla Quintet	Advert in *Sounds*, 21 August 1982

Weekend No.	Date	Bands	Notes and Source for the Event or Gig
25	Sunday 22 August	Subhumans The Mob A-Heads Pagans	Flyer exists
—	Sunday 29 August		
—	Sunday 5 September		
—	Saturday 11 September	Alien Brains Bladder Flask	Advert in *Sounds*, 11 September 1982
—	Friday 3 to Sunday 5 December	Andy Mason Units and The Ftuts, Closer To The Sun, Joe Fitzgerald, Errol Clark Trio, Osha, Philip John-Lee, Lol Coxhill, Double Helix, Dave Holland, Louis 'Fingers' O'Neil, ZigZag, Arnold Brown, Perry Benson, Bob Flag, Joanna Daily, The Lost Jockey, John Lane and Lea Nicholson, Fran Landesman, 2121 In The Metro, Miles Davis, Eastern Alliance, Podomoffski, Blanca Bartos, Eduardo Niebla	Flyer exists—confirmed by Eduardo Niebla. Advert in *Sounds*, 4 December 1982 but only mentions "Andy Mason Units and The Ftuts, Closer To The Sun"—band name was actually Towards The Sun, Eduardo Niebla's band Poster indicates it was a three-day festival "tickets £2 or £5 for 3 days" running 6:00–12:00 p.m. on Friday, 2:00 p.m.–12:00 a.m. on Saturday, 1:00 p.m.–12:00 a.m. on Sunday The assumption is that the names 'Miles Davis' and 'Dave Holland' on the poster were either jokes or were used by local bands as band names. The answer is lost to history.
1983	Sunday *unknown Date*	The Mob Null and Void Fracture The Omega Tribe	Potential 'farewell show' to Centro Iberico for the punks with the remaining squat residents removing their property ready for demolition. Described by Al Puppy in an article but no other evidence or memories exist

KNOWN CENTRO IBERICO EVENTS—
PRE-ALTERNATIVE CENTRE (1978–1981)

Year	Date	Bands	Notes and Source for the Event or Gig
1978	Saturday 21 October	Rudi Raped The A.U.M. Band	Flyer exists
1978	Sunday 5 November	Rudi Four Kings Bitch	Confirmed by Brian Young of Rudi—*NME* and *Sounds* listings exist
1978	Saturday 11 November	Public meeting and joint Anglo-Spanish social to mark Anarchist Day	Printed listings exist
1979	Sunday 21 January	Throbbing Gristle	Two flyers and the ticket exist 3pm, £1—P-Orridge states there was an audience of around 180. The full set was 'Persuasion', 'Day Song', 'Five Knuckle Shuffle' and 'Wall of Sound'
1979	*unknown*	Eduardo Niebla's first performance at Centro Iberico prior to being invited to move in	
1979	Saturday 6 October	All-night party to celebrate Joe Hill's hundredth birthday anniversary	Printed listings exist
1979	Friday 7 to Sunday 9 December	Anarcho-feminist conference	Included a meeting on 'Sex in the Anarchist Movement' held at Conway Hall on Saturday 8th
1979	*unknown*	The Lines	
1980	Friday 14 March	Poison Girls Disco Students Eratics	Flyer exists
1980	Saturday 29 March	Film showing of Buñuel's *Ensayo de un crimen* (*The Criminal Life of Archibaldo de la Cruz*) plus *Mr. and Mrs. Kabal's Theatre*, film by W. Borowcyk	Flyer exists—confirmed by Eduardo Niebla

Year	Date	Bands	Notes and Source for the Event or Gig
1980	Sunday 30 March	Eduardo Niebla Band Two-part performance consisting of (1) Roots on a Path—Communication and Dialogue for Several Instruments performed by Eduardo Niebla's band (2) Towards the Sun	Flyer exists—confirmed by Eduardo Niebla Towards the Sun was also Eduardo Niebla's band
1980	Saturday 10 May	Inner City Unit Androids Of Mu The Door and the Window	Flyer exists Side A of The Door and the Window's 1980 cassette, *Music And Movement*, was recorded at this gig
1980	Sunday 11 May	The Astronauts Zounds Drunken Poets	Flyer exists
1980	Saturday 26 July	2nd annual Peña Portobello Fiesta de la Poesía y la Música—incl. Jose Martin Artajo and Eduardo Niebla	Flyer exists
1980	Saturday 4 October	Eduardo Niebla and Friends	Flyer exists—confirmed by Eduardo Niebla
1981	Unknown, circa June	Torch Song	
1981	Saturday 20 June	3rd annual Peña Portobello Fiesta de la Poesía y la Música—incl. Eduardo Niebla and John Williams	Flyer exists—confirmed by Eduardo Niebla
1981	Tuesday 14 July	Eric Random Swamp Children The Wind Up Ensemble	Flyer exists The Wind Up Ensemble were Torch Song under a pseudonym
1981	Saturday 29 August	Zounds The Mob The Astronauts Null and Void	Flyer exists

KNOWN GIGS AT THE AUTONOMY CENTRE (OCTOBER 1981–FEBRUARY 1982)

Year	Date	Bands	Notes and Source for the Event or Gig
1981	Sunday 18 Oct	The Apostles Cold War Twelve Cubic Feet What Is Oil?	Mentioned in *Freedom* Confirmed in the gig listing included with The Apostles' second EP
1981	Sunday 22 Nov	Terminal Disaster Cold War Anabolic Steroids Urban Dissidents Flack Assassins Of Hope	Confirmed by Kill Your Pet Puppy
1981	Friday 27 Nov	JJ and the Flyers The Bat Band	Printed listing exists
1981	Sunday 29 Nov		
1981	Sunday 6 Dec	Hagar the Womb Luz y Fuerza The Apostles Null and Void The Mob, Zounds	Kill Your Pet Puppy Also confirmed in the gig listing included with The Apostles' second EP
1981	Sunday 13 Dec	Rudimentary Peni Cold War Assassins of Hope Primal Chaos Epsilons Cold War Flack Warning Screaming Babies	Michael Clarke confirmed via his diary but Sean Forbes and Rudimentary Peni believe The Anabolic Steroids also played
1981	Saturday 19 Dec	Crass DIRT	Kill Your Pet Puppy and the gagsdirt.co.uk site
1981	Sunday 20 Dec	Twelve Cubic Feet What Is Oil? The Apostles The Survivors	Recording shown on Discogs Also confirmed in the gig listing included with The Apostles' second EP

Year	Date	Bands	Notes and Source for the Event or Gig
1981	Sunday 27 Dec	The Sinyx Assassins of Hope Flack Boiled Eggs Cold War The Anabolic Steroids The Apostles	Flyer exists The gig listing with The Apostles' second EP in 1983 listed '86 Mix' instead of The Sinyx and also included The Anabolic Steroids and The Apostles
1981	Thursday 31 Dec	The Mob The Apostles Null and Void Flack Blood and Roses Turd Burglars Warning	The gig listing included with The Apostles' second EP mentions Warning but not Flack or the Turd Burglars
1982	Sunday 3 Jan	Part One Blood and Roses The Witches The Apostles The Committed	Kill Your Pet Puppy Paul May's 1982 gig list says The Committed played
1982	Sunday 10 Jan	Hagar the Womb Vertical Hold Faction Toucans Windy Miller and the Windmills Flack	Mick Slaughter confirmed Paul May's 1982 gig list confirmed
1982	Sunday 17 Jan	Conflict Rubella Ballet Faction Epsilons Seething Wells Anthrax	Mick Slaughter confirmed Paul May's 1982 gig list confirmed Nicholas Bullen believes Anthrax also played or were on a flyer
1982	Sunday 24 Jan	Rudimentary Peni Part 1 Slaughtered Innocence What Is Oil? Ex People The Void	Sean Forbes confirmed, poster is visible on the wall at the Autonomy Centre in a photo by Mickey Penguin
1982	Sunday 31 Jan	Anthrax Annie Anxiety DIRT Polemic Attack Social Diseases Youth In Asia	A flyer exists but only shows Annie Anxiety and Polemic Attack Mick Slaughter confirmed Paul May's 1982 gig list confirmed
1982	Sunday 7 Feb	The Snipers Cold War Faction The Assassins of Hope	Two flyers exist

Year	Date	Bands	Notes and Source for the Event or Gig
1982	Sunday 14 Feb	The Absconded Naked Chronic Outbursts The Condemned Locusts Jim Face and the Farmers	Paul May's 1982 gig list confirmed Nicholas Bullen confirms The Locusts were billed but did not play
1982	Sunday 21 Feb	Youth in Asia Flack The Committed The S-Haters Empty Dreams	Flyer exists—final show Nicholas Bullen confirms Empty Dreams played, while a further flyer lists Rudimentary Peni as the headliner but it seems they were for the 27 Feb
X	Saturday 27 Feb	The Sinyx Rudimentary Peni Epsilons	Flyer exists Cancelled—venue closed to gigs
X	Sunday 28 Feb	Ex People Flack Anthrax Smegma	Flyer exists Cancelled—venue closed to gigs
X	*unknown* March–April	The Subhumans Gambit of Shame The Mob Zounds Blood and Roses Hagar the Womb The Apostles 12 Cubic Feet The Godless Pinkoes	Flyer exists listing bookings for March–April Cancelled—venue closed to gigs

DISCOGRAPHY

Title	Notes	Release
Throbbing Gristle—At Centro Iberico, London	Released as part of the band's cassette series documenting every TG performance and since reissued on CD	September 1979
The Door and the Window—Music and Movement	Tracks 1–3 (Sticks and Stones, Death Looks Down, We Do Scare Each Other) recorded live on 10 May 1980	
An Odd Acts Event	Live compilation documenting excerpts of the May 1982 show	1982
Conflict—Live at Centro Iberico	Six-song 7" documenting the August 1982 show	1982
Ramleh/Libertarian Recordings—A Return to Slavery/Slaughter at Random	Side B is Consumer Electronics' June 1982 show; Philip Best had joined Whitehouse and didn't want to use the CE name	1983
Centro Iberico, London, May 1982	In September 2025, Susan Lawly, the label run by former Whitehouse frontman William Bennett, released a short excerpt on YouTube showing the playground, entrance and ground floor hall of Centro Iberico. The clip was taken from an unknown 1982 VHS release from Come Organisation, Whitehouse's then label.	1982
Whitehouse—Live Action 6/ Live Action 33	Live Action 6 is the June 1982 show mislabelled as 19 July	1984

Unofficial recordings exist in the hands of a number of tapers who were present including Mick Slaughter and Sean Forbes. Thank you to Mick and Sean for kindly allowing me to confirm additional dates with them

NOTES

PREFACE

1   Discussion saved in Hansard, the official report of all Parliamentary debates: Homelessness, HL Deb 25 June 1975, vol. 361, cc1516–54, accessed June 2025, https://api.parliament.uk/historic-hansard/lords/1975/jun/25/homelessness.

2   "At Least 354,000 People Homeless in England Today," Shelter, 11 December 2024, accessed June 2025, https://england.shelter.org.uk/media/press_release/at_least_354000_people_homeless_in_england_today_; Evolve Housing + Support "Facts About Homelessness In London" at https://www.evolvehousing.org.uk/learn-and-share/10-facts-about-homelessness-london/.

3   (Black Dog, 1999), pp. 0.9 and 9.4.

4   I'm heartened that poking at this subject seems to have provoked an overdue upgrade in June 2025.

5   According to Albert Meltzer's highly recommended autobiography, *I Couldn't Paint Golden Angels*, Meltzer warned García that Soper was a fervent advocate of teetotalism, to which García responded: "I know priests. You don't have to tell me, a Spaniard, about these holy fathers, as they call themselves. I will offer him a glass of wine, and he will agree to everything." Luckily, Soper left the group in peace and the idea remained untested (AK Press, 1996), 211.

BORN OF STRUGGLE, LIVING IN HOPE

1   The Spanish confederation of anarcho-syndicalist labour unions. García's father also acted as bodyguard to Salvador Seguí Rubinat, secretary of the union, who was ultimately assassinated by gunmen working for the local body representing Catalan employers.

2   Confederación Nacional del Trabajo (CNT) and Federacion Anarquista Iberica (Iberian Anarchist Federation) respectively. CNT-FAI is a common abbreviation due to the strong overlap between the two organisations, with members of the latter taking over the leadership of the CNT by the mid-1930s.

3   Five hundred thousand Spaniards crossed into France with 60,000 joining the French army. In the defence of France, around 6,000 gave their lives. Then, with Franco's quiet approval, 7,500 wound up as inmates at Mauthausen concentration camp where two-thirds of them would

die. Authorities in Vichy France employed 220,000 Spaniards as forced labour and from among their ranks, experienced antifascists would form a significant cadre within the Maquis and the Free French Army. The key hope of the Spanish fighters was that support would be rewarded by Allied action against Fascist Spain, a hope soon crushed.

FREEDOM

1 An acronym of Basque Euskadi Ta Askatasuna, 'Basque Homeland and Liberty.'
2 His sentencing alongside co-conspirator Fernando Carballo followed on 3 September, with Christie receiving a twenty-year sentence and Carballo thirty. Carballo would languish in prison until 13 January 1977.
3 *Direct Action* 9, no. 2, February 1968.

SECOND LIVES

1 Freedom Press Hall at 84B Whitechapel High Street remains the home of Freedom Press to this day. The press notice appeared in *Freedom* 31, no. 5, 14 February 1970.
2 *Bulletin of the Anarchist Black Cross* I, no. 8 June 1970.
3 Police raided Christie's home on 27 February 1968 and 11 June 1970, looking for explosives. From early January 1971, he was the subject of a police manhunt backed by a vitriolic press campaign.
4 A precursor to the more famous trial was the arrest of Jack Prescott on 19 January 1971, his re-arrest (along with a Dutch friend, Jan Oudenaarden, who would be released) on 11 February, then the arrest of Ian Purdie on 6 March. Both would be charged with responsibility for Angry Brigade bombings only for Purdie to be found not guilty on 1 December, while Prescott was found not guilty of any specific actions but did receive fifteen years for conspiracy to cause bombings.
5 Christie's account is repeated in Gordon Carr, *The Angry Brigade: A History of Britain's First Urban Guerrilla Group* (PM Press, 2010).

FINDING COMMUNITY

1 The exact date of publication is unknown, but the pamphlet was advertised for sale in the June 1970 issue of the *Bulletin of the Anarchist Black Cross.*
2 *Black Flag* II, no. 5, May 1971.
3 Quico, Manolo, and Pepe Sabaté were key postwar guerrillas with a particular talent for eye-catching acts of resistance which earned them notoriety. Pepe would be killed in 1949, Quico in 1960. Manolo was arrested in 1949 and, due to his surname, was subject to the death penalty.
4 Peirats's success was reported in *Black Flag* II, no. 6, June 1971.
5 Kavanagh edited an agitator newssheet, *Ludd*, during the 1966 seamen's strike bringing him into Meltzer's circle. The two formed the Coptic Press imprint at 7 Coptic Street by the British Museum, where they would also employ Christie. Going by the change in contact details in *Black Flag*, by March 1969 that address had closed and the publishing ventures, along with the Anarchist Black Cross, headed to 735 Fulham Road before the Anarchist Black Cross arrived at 10 Gilbert Place in January 1970.

6   *Black Flag* III, no. 3, June 1973.

ANARCHY ESTABLISHED … AND DISESTABLISHED
1   'Spotlight On London's Anarchist Spaces: Centro Iberico,' Past Tense, 5 March 2021, https://pasttense.co.uk/2021/03/05/spotlight-on-londons-historical-anarchist-spaces-centro-iberico/.
2   *Black Flag* IV, no. 1, May 1975.
3   *Black Flag* III, no. 8, January 1974: "… in support of political prisoners *Anarchist Cabaret* February 2nd and 16th; *Cabaret of the Minorities 'Gai Chansons'* February 9th and 23rd."
4   Olday took part in the revolts in Germany toward the end of the First World War, then opposed the Nazis before fleeing to London in 1938. Working in continental resistance circles, he refused conscription, continued to illustrate anarchist materials while in hiding, and was finally arrested. After the war, he remained active on all fronts until his death in London in the summer of 1977. Olday did not get on with García, though he was permitted to restage old Hamburg cabaret shows at Centro Iberico, and the centre advertised plans to exhibit his paintings (*Black Flag* III, no. 8, January 1974).
5   *Freedom* 37, no. 14, 10 July 1976. *Black Flag* IV, no. 10, September 1976 provided the official statement regarding the closure with *Black Flag* IV, no. 11, November 1976 announcing the next move.
6   The Jacksons Lane Arts Centre thrives to this day. Thanks are due to Max Smiles and the team at Jacksons Lane for their assistance while creating this book.

NO POINT IN ASKING
1   *Black Flag* IV, no. 14, February 1977. The "Listen Punks" article by Philip Ruff (writing as Henry Black) made a shrewd comparison between Lydon and Mick Jagger, stating, "Perhaps Johnny Rotten will climb the same ladder to tax-evading seclusion as part of the musical establishment too."
2   *Black Flag* IV, no. 15, 1977. *Black Flag* temporarily stopped dating issues in 1977.

NEW MOVES
1   *Freedom* 38, no. 23, 26 November 1977, then confirmed by *Black Flag* 5, no. 2, 1977—the latter written somewhere amid the six weeks from 27 October to 10 December.
2   Thank you to Oliver Jones and the team at City of Westminster Archives for their support.
3   The Derelicts broke up in 1976, evolving into The Passions, while The 101ers ceased in May 1976, evolving into The Clash.

NO FUTURE / A FUTURE
1   *Black Flag* V, no. 6, October 1978. One oddity from the same period is that the Spanish Ministry of Labour and Immigration lists an unknown 1978 publication, *El Lince: Boletín de la Emigración* (The lynx: immigration newsletter), which it credits to 'Centro Iberico (London).'

2 The Special Branch's annual report for 1978, dated 31 January 1979, lists the AUM as one of several anarchist groups infiltrated by undercover police. The group itself was long-standing, with confirmed meetings at the London School of Economics as early as 1977 and as late as 1982, when it met every Thursday at 8 p.m. at the Half-Way House pub opposite Camden Town tube station.

3 Conning confirms that The Lines' show was "around the time of our first Peel session" (live session on John Peel's show on BBC Radio One), which took place on Tuesday 8 January 1980, suggesting a late 1979 gig.

4 Others also recall the involvement of 'Spanish Elizabeth' with Centro Iberico before she went on to help convert a number of squatted properties into the Brougham Road Housing Cooperative in 1982 and 1983. Andy Martin remembers: "being on the top floor of the Centro Iberico with Elizabeth—dark-haired, very tall—translating for a gentleman with fairly thick horn-rimmed glasses and slicked-back grey hair and occasional lapses into English with a very heavy Spanish accent, but mainly speaking in Spanish."

5 *Freedom* 40, no 23, 22 December 1979. The *London Workers' Group Bulletin* no. 6, 1979, also advertised the celebration for Joe Hill.

6 Presumably, there had been a first in 1979, though the date is unknown.

PERSONS UNKNOWN

1 *Black Flag* IV, no. 3, August 1975.

2 Ladd had previously been jailed in 1973 for planting hoax bombs at two Portuguese vice consulates.

3 The police were also required to return the 'explosives' found at Mills' address to her: two bags of sugar, one and a half bags of flour, and two tins of weedkiller.

4 An account is given in a Special Branch report dated 30 November 1978: https://www.ucpi.org.uk/wp-content/uploads/2021/04/UCPI0000013011.pdf.

5 For example, a night of Irish folk music at the Woodpecker Pub in Leeds raised £54.

6 While sometimes referred to as an 'anarchist centre,' a space set up at 109 Back Church Lane in 1977–1978 was ultimately just an office. The groups responsible, the Zero Collective and Anarchy Collective, fell into dispute with the former dissolving in 1978 and the latter dwindling to a handful of members.

OPTIMISM AND AUTONOMY

1 *Freedom* 41, no. 10, 24 May 1980.

2 *Black Flag* VI, no. 3, (no month given) 1980.

3 *Freedom* 41, no. 25, 20 December 1980.

4 *Freedom* 42, no. 11, 6 June 1981.

5 In 1981, A Distribution's official address was 182 Upper Street, the Rising Free bookshop, while Little A Press was based in Metropolitan Wharf. Several of the individuals involved were squatting St James's Church on Pentonville Road, which had been built in 1787 and closed in 1977,

whereupon it became a squat until its demolition in 1984. It was referred to, apparently interchangeably, as 'the Parallel Universe' or 'the Grimaldi church' (due to the famous clown performer buried in the graveyard.)

6   *Freedom* 42, no. 20, 10 October 1981. Working backwards quarterly from the confirmed date of 22 March, rent would have been due on 22 December, 22 September, and 22 June.

7   A long-term survivor of the Autonomy Centre is the London Anarchist Bookfair. Research by The Sparrow's Nest confirms that the Big A Sale was the first, though its less-than-sparkling success meant there was no repeat in 1982. The next was organised by A Distribution at a pub in Kings Cross on 26 November 1983 and it has run ever since.

8   Albert Meltzer, *I Couldn't Paint Golden Angels: Sixty Years of Commonplace Life and Anarchist Agitation* (AK Press, 1996), 298.

9   Michael Clarke writing at https://shit-fi.com/reviews/IntheOldDays and with the author over email.

10 The A Collective continued to operate from Metropolitan Wharf thereafter.

BEGINNINGS AND ENDINGS

1   A riff on Patti Smith's 'Ghost Dance' apparently. See the flyer by Tony Drayton and essays by Alistair Livingston (Al Puppy) here https://killyourpetpuppy.co.uk/news/subway-surfing-anarcho-goths/.

2   Miguel García and Albert Meltzer, eds., *Miguel García's Story* (The Miguel García Memorial Committee and Cienfuegos Press, 1982); *Black Flag* VI, no. 10, January 1982, and VI, no. 11, May 1982; *Freedom* 19 December 1981. Discogs indicates The Apostles demo was recorded 13–14 March 1982: https://www.discogs.com/release/20518315-The-Apostles-The-Second-Demo-13-140382.

3   Opened in 1912 as the 1,250-capacity Grand Cinema, it was bombed out in World War Two and then rebuilt in 1955–1956. The building became the Essoldo Bingo Club from 1966 until its closure.

LET'S START A WAR...

1   In *Sounds* 2 January 1982, in a piece entitled 'Wrath of the Racists' Bushell argued: "It shows who the BM think are their real enemies, not the hippy *NME* but bands like the Upstarts and journalists who answer the BM's vicious propaganda by relating to the kids whose minds they're trying to poison."

DIY ODD ACTS

1   See the entry at 'Lady June,' Calyx: The Canterbury Music Website, accessed 5 July 2025, http://www.calyx-canterbury.fr/mus/june_lady.html; and at 'Various: An Odd Acts Event,' Discogs accessed 5 July 2025, https://www.discogs.com/release/2328085-Various-An-Odd-Acts-Event.

2   Wendy Jones and Grayson Perry, *Portrait of the Artist as a Young Girl* (Vintage, 2007), 175–77. Perry states the performance took place in Brixton. Given that Neo-Naturists apparently did a show in Brixton that same day, the confusion is explainable.

WEEKENDS OF ACTION

1   It appears that the weekends in question were those beginning Friday 21 May, Friday 28 May, and Friday 4 June.

2   The 5 June cancellation and 12 June gig were accidentally misdated as July on Whitehouse 'Live Action' releases, the latter was also misdated as 19 June in one source. Presumably a simple misreading of notes on old cassettes, extant sources confirm the true dates. Beyond the fact that the 5, 12, and 19 July were all Mondays, *Sounds* advertised both performances in gig listings. Meanwhile, the Consumer Electronics' performance was released in 1983 as 'Slaughter at Random' under the name Libertarian Recordings, with liner notes indicating it was recorded on 12 June and then mixed on 26 June.

3   *Freedom* 43, no. 8, 1 May 1982. Also in *Freedom* on 17 April, 29 May, and 12 June. Meltzer's tribute appeared in *Black Flag* VI, no. 10, January 1982.

4   The weekend event took place, likely not coincidentally, with the week-long festivities of 1982 Gay Pride Week as part of which Wendy Wattage performed nightly at Oval House from 24 to 27 June. Ellis had lived in two properties on Railton Road in the 1970s where the South London Gay Liberation group were neighbours to and collaborators with an anarchist news service, a claimants' union, the Brixton Advice Centre, Icebreakers (a gay counselling group), the National Gay News Defence Committee, the Race Today Collective, two women's centres, and various squatter support services.

MOBS, POETS, SINYX, AND WINDMILLS

1   'Autonomy Centres, Riots & the Big Rammy,' *Uncarved*, accessed 5 July 2025, https://www.uncarved.org/music/apunk/autcent.html.

2   The tape was recorded by Chris Low and can be heard on the Kill Your Pet Puppy website: https://killyourpetpuppy.co.uk/news/the-apostles-centro-iberico-westbourne-park-london-w11-130802/.

3   Gregory Bull and Mickey Penguin, *Not Just Bits of Paper* (Earth Island Books, 2014).

THE END

1   Papers are held in the City of Westminster Archives. The *Marylebone Mercury*, Friday 30 March 1984 announced the official opening and Livingstone's presence. 421 Harrow Road is currently occupied by the Paddington Law Centre offering free, specialist legal support to the vulnerable and destitute.

2   The addresses in question included 103 Grosvenor Avenue, numbers 53 and 59 Cross Street, and 109 Corbyn Street. The collective would survive until 2002.

ABOUT THE AUTHOR

Nick Soulsby is the author of *Everything Keeps Dissolving: Conversations with Coil* (2022); *Lydia Lunch: The War Is Never Over* (2019); *Swans: Sacrifice and Transcendence* (2018); *Thurston Moore: We Sing a New Language* (2017); *Cobain on Cobain: Interviews & Encounters* (2016); *I Found My Friends: The Oral History of Nirvana* (2015); and *Dark Slivers: Seeing Nirvana in the Shards of Incesticide* (2012). In 2026 two new works by Soulsby will be published: *Viva Negativa! The New Blockaders, Anti Art and Noise 1982–2025* and a comprehensive biography of Peter 'Sleazy' Christopherson.

ABOUT PM PRESS

PM Press is an independent, radical publisher of critically necessary books for our tumultuous times. Our aim is to deliver bold political ideas and vital stories to all walks of life and arm the dreamers to demand the impossible. Founded in 2007 by a small group of people with decades of publishing, media, and organizing experience, we have sold millions of copies of our books, most often one at a time, face to face. We're old enough to know what we're doing and young enough to know what's at stake. Join us to create a better world.

PM Press
PO Box 23912
Oakland, CA 94623
www.pmpress.org

PM Press in Europe
europe@pmpress.org
www.pmpress.org.uk

FRIENDS OF PM PRESS

These are indisputably momentous times—the
financial system is melting down globally and the
Empire is stumbling. Now more than ever there is a
vital need for radical ideas.

In the many years since its founding—and on a mere
shoestring—PM Press has risen to the formidable challenge of publishing
and distributing knowledge and entertainment for the struggles ahead. With
hundreds of releases to date, we have published an impressive and stimulating
array of literature, art, music, politics, and culture. Using every available
medium, we've succeeded in connecting those hungry for ideas and information
to those putting them into practice.

Friends of PM allows you to directly help impact, amplify, and revitalize the
discourse and actions of radical writers, filmmakers, and artists. It provides us
with a stable foundation from which we can build upon our early successes and
provides a much-needed subsidy for the materials that can't necessarily pay
their own way. You can help make that happen—and receive every new title
automatically delivered to your door once a month—by joining as a Friend of
PM Press. And, we'll throw in a free T-shirt when you sign up.

Here are your options:

- **$30 a month** Get all books and pamphlets plus a 50% discount on all
  webstore purchases

- **$40 a month** Get all PM Press releases (including CDs and DVDs) plus a
  50% discount on all webstore purchases

- **$100 a month** Superstar—Everything plus PM merchandise, free downloads,
  and a 50% discount on all webstore purchases

For those who can't afford $30 or more a month, we have **Sustainer Rates** at
$15, $10 and $5. Sustainers get a free PM Press T-shirt and a 50% discount on
all purchases from our website.

Your Visa or Mastercard will be billed once a month, until you tell us to stop.
Or until our efforts succeed in bringing the revolution around. Or the financial
meltdown of Capital makes plastic redundant. Whichever comes first.

Spanish Punk: Screaming for Democracy in a Postdictatorial State

David Vila Diéguez with a Foreword by Isabela Raygoza

ISBN: 9798887441047
$25.95   240 pages

What does democracy sound like when it's shouted through a distortion pedal?

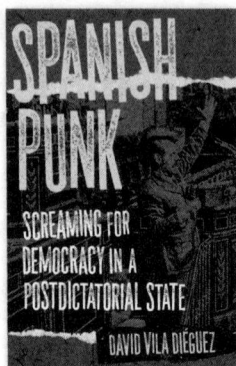

In 1975, Spain emerged from the long shadow of Franco's dictatorship, stumbling toward democracy amid uncertainty, unrest, and unhealed wounds. In the same moment, a raw, raucous, and radically irreverent cultural force exploded onto the scene: punk.

Spanish Punk: Screaming for Democracy in a Postdictatorial State is the first in-depth study to trace the uniquely political trajectory of punk in post-Franco Spain. Far from just a musical genre, Spanish punk became a rebellious cultural matrix—a defiant, DIY response to the contradictions of a state trying to reinvent itself. Through fanzines, lyrics, testimonies, and subcultural style, punks posed urgent questions: What kind of democracy was being built? Who was being left out? And how do you scream dissent in a newly "free" society?

Blending historical, philosophical, musicological, and textual analysis, this book shows how punk served as both a glue for oppositional movements and a generator of alternative political identities. It's a long-overdue exploration of how cultural resistance helped shape a generation's answer to dictatorship—and its uneasy aftermath.

"Spanish Punk is a well-researched and laid out study of a subculture that has resonated with people around the world. How punk found a foothold amidst the Spanish political climate of the '80s is an important chapter in its history and will not be forgotten thanks to David Vila Diéguez."
—Shawna Potter, front-person for War On Women and author of *Making Spaces Safer: A Guide to Giving Harassment the Boot Wherever You Work, Play, and Gather*

"A fine journey through a misunderstood and ignored punk epoch that needs a searchlight just like this to illuminate the cultural concerns and political issues, regional conflicts and fragmented history. With a knack for both academic insight and observational detail, seen in a lens on La Polla Records and others. Spanish Punk is must-have for those seeking to understand how punk unfolded in a crises ridden time and place struggling to escape the throes of fascism."
—David Ensminger, author of *Left of the Dial: Conversations with Punk Icons*

This Is a Message to Persons Unknown: The Story of Poison Girls

Rich Cross with Alec Dunn and Erin Yanke

ISBN: 979-8-88744-136-8 (paperback)
       979-8-88744-144-3 (hardcover)
$34.95/$69.95   320 pages

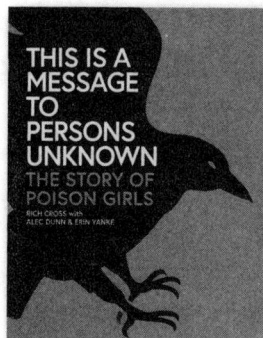

Flesh and blood are what we are, flesh and blood are who we are, our cover is blown ...

This Is a Message to Persons Unknown is the first full history of the legendary band Poison Girls. From their first gigs in Brighton in 1977 to years of DIY tours across Britain and Europe, the band forged a radical path through music, politics, and art.

Fronted by the uncompromising Vi Subversa—a singular lyricist, songwriter, and voice—Poison Girls challenged punk's Year Zero myth, weaving ferocity with wit, emotional depth, and inventive sound. Just as formative to anarcho-punk as Crass, yet defiantly their own, Poison Girls confronted misogyny, ageism, and authoritarianism with a passion and clarity that still resonates today.

Drawing on exclusive interviews, zines, contemporary accounts, and the personal archives of band members, this richly illustrated history documents Poison Girls' unforgettable songs, striking graphics, and fierce campaigns of resistance.

More than just a band biography, *This Is a Message to Persons Unknown* tells the story of a group of dissident artists who turned punk into both a protest and a possibility—an experiment in living, creating, and fighting for something new.

"Why the fuck did I have a Crass shirt in high school but didn't hear about their peers, Poison Girls, until recently? When we do the meaningful work of digging back through the past and shining a light on women artists, we are making right past wrongs. Legendary all-male bands are only legendary because we gave them proper attention (sometimes exaggerated and undeserved) at the time, allowing their status to grow and their contributions to be oversold. But when women-centric bands are ignored or dismissed while active, their contributions not valued, it says less about their abilities in comparison to their peers and more about the insidiousness of sexism. Who else is missing from the history books? This Is a Message to Persons Unknown *ensures Poison Girls will not be forgotten."*
—Shawna Potter, front-person for War On Women and author of *Making Spaces Safer: A Guide to Giving Harassment the Boot Wherever You Work, Play, and Gather*

The Day the Country Died: A History of Anarcho Punk 1980–1984

Ian Glasper

ISBN: 978-1-60486-516-5
$24.95   496 pages

The Day the Country Died features author, historian, and musician Ian Glasper (*Burning Britain*) exploring in minute detail the influential, esoteric, UK anarcho punk scene of the early Eighties. If the colorful '80s punk bands captured in *Burning Britain* were loud, political, and uncompromising, those examined in *The Day the Country Died* were even more so, totally prepared to risk their liberty to communicate the ideals they believed in so passionately.

With Crass and Poison Girls opening the floodgates, the arrival of bands such as Zounds, Flux of Pink Indians, Conflict, Subhumans, Chumbawamba, Amebix, Rudimentary Peni, Antisect, Omega Tribe, and Icons of Filth heralded a brand new age of honesty and integrity in underground music. With a backdrop of Thatcher's Britain, punk music became self-sufficient and considerably more aggressive, blending a DIY ethos with activism to create the perfectly bleak soundtrack to the zeitgeist of a discontented British youth.

It was a time when punk stopped being merely a radical fashion statement, and became a force for real social change; a genuine revolutionary movement, driven by some of the most challenging noises ever committed to tape. Anarchy, as regards punk rock, no longer meant "cash from chaos." It meant "freedom, peace, and unity." Anarcho punk took the rebellion inherent in punk from the beginning to a whole new level of personal awareness.

All the scene's biggest names, and most of the smaller ones, are comprehensively covered with new, exclusive interviews and hundreds of previously unseen photographs.

"The oral testimony assembled here provides an often-lucid participant's view of the work of the wider anarcho-punk milieu, which demonstrates just as tellingly the diversity as well as the commonality by which it was defined. The collection hints at the extent to which—within a militant antiwar, anti-work, anti-system framework— the perception and priorities of the movement's activists differed: something the movement's critics (who were always keen to deride the uniformity of the 'Crass punks') rarely understood."
—Rich Cross, *Freedom*

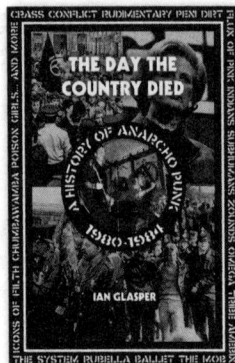